WHAT READERS HAVE

MW00572703

THE UNCOUNTED IRISH IN CANADA AND THE UNITED STATES
(Fitzgerald & King), several chapters of which appear in IRELAND TO
NORTH AMERICA *in amended and improved form:*

"...an important book that should be in any good university library...the authors deal with documentary evidence rather than accept uncritically the theories that have mystified the position of the Irish in the United States." – historian Donald H. Akenson, Queen's University, Kingston, Ontario, in *Canadian Review of Studies in Nationalism.*

"Done gently with feeling and care...a noble service...worth reading and worth having." – Prof. Stewart Donovan, *Atlantic Provinces Book Review.*

"The most significant contribution of their approach is the demonstration of the recurring importance of chain migration within family groups." – Prof. William J. Smyth, St. Patrick's College, Maynooth, in *Canadian Journal of Irish Studies.*

"...a text for those who want their history as interesting narrative, rather than dry-dust composition." – Michael O. Nowlan, *Atlantic Advocate.*

"...readable...academically respectable...fairly imposing bibliographies...good indexes." – *Books Ireland.*

"...breaks new ground in the history of Irish immigration." – *Irish Herald*, San Francisco.

"...a basic text for charting the arrival and influence of ethnic groups in this country and Canada." – Diane Donovan, *Midwest Book Review.*

"...a colorful collage and sweep of history...a fascinating blend of history and genealogy." – Bernard H. Broderick, *Northumberland News.*

"...use of 'case studies' analysis of genealogical records and census data to prove various points is well done, and should be a model for other writers." – historian Robert Ryal Miller, Berkeley, California.

Irish History & Emigration Series

Edited by Joseph A. King

also by Joseph A. King

The Irish Lumberman-Farmer (1982)
Lithuanian Families of Luzerne Co., Pennsylvania (1986)
The Uncounted Irish in Canada and the United States,
    with Margaret E. Fitzgerald (1990)
Captain Thomas Fallon of Santa Cruz,
    San Jose, and San Francisco (monograph, 1990)
Winter of Entrapment: A New Look at
    the Donner Party (1992)
A Unique Parish (1994)

Irish History & Emigration Series

Volume 1

Ireland to North America

emigrants from West Cork

by

Joseph A. King

K&K PUBLICATIONS
Lafayette, California
&
P. D. MEANY PUBLISHERS
Toronto

ISBN 0-9608500-8-2 (United States)

Library of Congress Catalog Card Number: 94-77047

Canadian Cataloguing in Publication Data
King, Joseph A., 1925-
Ireland to North America: Emigrants from West Cork
(Irish history & emigration series: v. 1)
Rev. chapters from: The Uncounted Irish in Canada and the United States.
Includes bibliog. references and index.
Canadian ISBN 0-88835-044-9.
1. Irish - United States - History - 19th century. 2. Irish - United States - Genealogy. 3. Irish Americans - History - 19th century. 4. Irish Americans - Genealogy. 5. Irish - New Brunswick - Miramichi Region - History - 19th century. 6. Irish - New Brunswick - Miramichi River Region - Genealogy. 7. United States - Emigration and Immigration - History - 19th century. 8. Miramichi River Region (N.B.) - Emigration and Immigration - History - 19th century. 9. Schull (Ireland) - Emigration - History - 19th century. I. Title. II. Series
E184.I6K5 1994   973'.0049162   C94-931802-7

Distributed in Ireland by:
Eason & Son Ltd., Brickfield Drive, Crumlin, Dublin 12
Schull Books, Ballydehob, Skibbereen, County Cork

Distributed in Canada by:
P.D. Meany Publishers, Box 118, Streetsville, Ontario L5M 2B7
Farrell McCarthy Books, 109 Roy Avenue, Newcastle, New
  Brunswick E1V 3N8

Distributed in the USA by:
BookWorld Services, Inc., 1933 Whitfield Loop, Sarasota, FL 34243
Irish Books & Media, 1433 Franklin Avenue East, Minneapolis, MN
55404-2135

Cover: Harrigan's Rocks in Toormore Bay, County Cork, Ireland,
            1982 photo by Betty Wayne King

Published in the U.S. by K&K Publications, Box 564, Lafayette, CA
94549.
Published in Canada by P.D. Meany Publishers, Box 118,
Streetsville, Ontario L5M 2B7.

Table of Contents

Illustrations

Preface

At least four volumes are planned for the *Irish History & Emigration Series*. The first of these, *Ireland to North America*, consists basically of several chapters from *The Uncounted Irish in Canada and the United States* (Fitzgerald & King), published in 1990, clothbound, but I have made a number of additions and improvements.

Ireland to North America is a story of emigration from a remote parish in Southwest Cork, focusing on a typical Irish family of the early 19th century. It describes their life in Ireland and follows their fortunes to New Brunswick, Canada, where family members learned the logging trade, then took their skills westward over the course of two or three generations, following the rivers and the pines, and later the railroads, into Maine, Wisconsin, Minnesota, and the Pacific Northwest.

In an earlier book, *The Irish Lumberman-Farmer* (1982), I called this the Northern Migration Route, long ignored by historians of immigration despite its importance. This path was further described in the aforementioned *The Uncounted Irish*, written with Dr. Margaret E. Fitzgerald of New York City.

Over the years I have been helped by many people. These include genealogists Dr. Gordon Vaughn of St. Paul and Jerry Brosious of Stillwater, Minnesota; Sue Collins of the Stillwater Public Library; Kitty Hobson of the Oshkosh Museum; and these New Brunswickers: Jack F. Connell and Fr. Bernard Broderick of the St. Michael's Museum Association in Chatham; Cathy Driscoll and the late Edith McAllister of the Old Manse Library in Newcastle; the late Brian and Frank Mahoney of Williamstown; the late Josephine King and her husband, John King, also deceased, of Nelson; Josephine and the late Basil Harrigan of Nelson; Doreen M. Arbuckle, now of Ottawa. My indebtedness to W.D. Hamilton, professor emeritus of the University of New Brunswick at Fredericton, for his historical and genealogical research on early New Brunswick (*Old North Esk Revised, Miramichi Papers,* and other works) and for his friendship is beyond measure. I want to thank also Farrell

McCarthy of Newcastle, New Brunswick, founding president of the Irish Canadian Cultural Association of New Brunswick, for his encouragement over many years; for the promotion and reviews of my books in the Association's newsletter, *The Shamrock Leaf*; and for the hospitality he and his wife Edna have extended me during several visits to the Miramichi.

Sources of much assistance in Ireland include Mary Margaret Lucey, Declan O'Mahoney, and Mike Donovan of Schull and Goleen parishes; Jack O'Connell of Schull Books and Jack Roberts of Key Books; Fr. Diarmuid O'Connor of Goleen and the late Fr. John Deasy of Schull. Tim Cadogan of the Cork County Library has been an especially helpful archivist. My chapter "A Parish in West Cork" for *The Uncounted Irish* (which re-appears in considerably revised form in this volume) was read in early manuscript form by Tim, as well as by Professor Patrick J. Corish of Maynooth, Fr. James Coombes of Skibbereen, Fr. Patrick Hickey of Drinagh; and a later version by Diarmuid Ó Murchadha of the Cork Historical & Archaeological Society. Their corrections and suggestions were invaluable; so were those of Patrick D. Meany, my Toronto publisher and a wise editor.

Scholars will often find references to the more arcane sources in the body of the text and, if not, in the bibliographical annotation.

My sister Margaret Elizabeth has provided much encouragement and help in matters of Irish history, including a critique of an early draft of this book. My wife of thirty-nine years, Betty Wayne, continues to be my patient instructor on the word processor and, as always, a superb editor. She watches carefully to see that I do not, in bouts of enthusiasm, make all of my Irish historical characters as grandiose as the mythic Cuchullain and Deirdre or as saintly as Patrick.

Joseph A. King
Walnut Creek, California
1994

in appreciation of my sister
Margaret Elizabeth
for fueling my interest in Irish history,
and of our beloved parents,
Joseph Anthony King Sr. (1892-1951)
and
Margaret Mary Fitzgerald (1899-1984),
who valued their Irish heritage

and in memory of all those on the Mizen Peninsula who
suffered and died during the Great Hunger

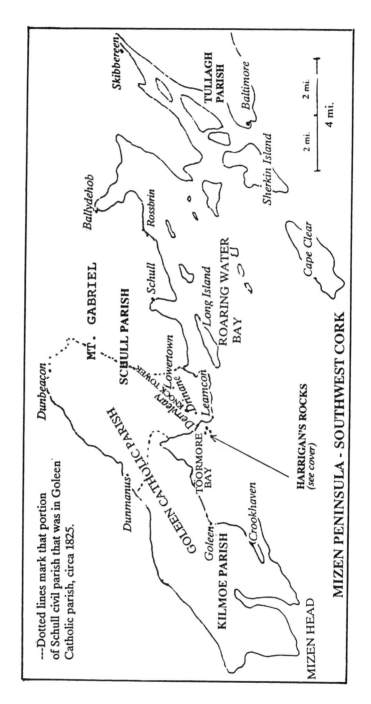

--Dotted lines mark that portion
of Schull civil parish that was in Goleen
Catholic parish, circa 1825.

MT. GABRIEL

SCHULL PARISH

Dunbeacon

GOLEEN CATHOLIC PARISH

Dunmanus

KILMOE PARISH

Goleen

Crookhaven

TOORMORE
BAY

MIZEN HEAD

Leamcon

Lowertown

Derryleary KNOCK TOWER

Dreenane

Schull

Ballydehob

Rossbrin

Long Island

ROARING WATER
BAY

Skibbereen

TULLAGH
PARISH

Baltimore

Sherkin Island

Cape Clear

HARRIGAN'S ROCKS
(see cover)

MIZEN PENINSULA - SOUTHWEST CORK

2 mi.   2 mi.

4 mi.

Chapter 1

Schull: A Parish in West Cork

from ancient times to the Great Famine

Mount Gabriel, on Ireland's southernmost peninsula, rises dramatically 1,339 feet above the rugged Cork coastline. From the top on a clear day one can view the mountains of Kerry and Cork to the west and north, the coastline east toward the city of Cork, and Clear Island to the south, where Irish is still spoken. Hundreds of thousands of Americans and Canadians have an Irish ancestor sprung perhaps five or six generations ago from the many parishes that can be spied from this mountaintop. For definition of terms used in this chapter, see Appendix B: Irish Terminology.

MIZEN PENINSULA ROOTS

With the significant fall in the price of Irish agricultural produce after the Battle of Waterloo and the Peace of 1815, an especially large group of emigrants began leaving southwest Cork. A popular migration route over the course of two or three generations ran from Cork to New Brunswick and Maine, and then westward to Michigan, Wisconsin, Minnesota, and the Pacific Northwest. Little has been written about their Canadian experience, and even less about the particular townlands and parishes from which these emigrants came, but if their descendants have in their family tree a surname like (O)Driscoll, (O)Mahony, (O)Donovan, (O)Regan, (O)Sullivan, (O)Daly, (O)Brien, (O)Coghlan, McCarthy, Hickey, Kingston, Goggin, Sauntry, Lucey, to name just a few, there is a good chance that the parish of their ancestor's birth can be viewed from Mount Gabriel's peak.

This is the story of one parish, Schull, also spelled "Skull" in the records, at the foot of Mount Gabriel on the Mizen Peninsula. It is not an exceptional story; it could be repeated for hundreds of parishes in Cork and elsewhere in Ireland. It is hoped that the story will offer some insight into just what life was like in Ireland and the New World for those who followed the route of emigration from Ireland to Canada, both before and after the Great Famine.

To tell that story we will follow the fortunes of the family of William Fitzgerald and his Harrigan in-laws. William appears on a United States census for the last time in 1870. In that year he and his spouse Ann Harrigan, ages given as 78 for both, although other records indicate they were even older, were living in the household of their daughter Kate McPartlin in Oshkosh, Wisconsin.

William and Ann were married in West Cork, probably in the Parish of Schull, about 1808. William was a carpenter and small farmer. He and Ann had at least eight children before emigrating to New Brunswick in 1830. There, with many relatives who joined them, they settled in remote Williamstown in North Esk Parish, Northumberland County (known as "Miramichi," for the river), cleared some land, and built log cabins. William and his older sons learned the skills of the logger in the woods and on the rivers. In 1833 and 1835, he and Ann had two more children, Kate and Ann. In 1855 they moved to Oshkosh, Wisconsin, where they spent their final years surrounded by children and grandchildren and other families who had followed the same path of emigration from the Mizen Peninsula in County Cork.

When William and Ann died in Oshkosh in 1873 and 1880 respectively, they left no written record of their life journey. No photographs or letters or Bible records have come down, but at least part of the story of their roots in Ireland can be told.

IRELAND

The story begins in a troubled land, in the townlands of Drinane and Derryleary, three miles southwest of the tiny port of Schull. There, among many close relatives, William Fitzgerald worked the marginal and mountainous soil, pursued the carpentry trade with his Harrigan in-laws, and harvested the seaweed used as a fertilizer and a food in famine times from Harrigan's Rocks in Toormore Bay. The weed cutting rights were leased from landlord Richard Edward Hull of Leamcon House, a short distance from their cabins. The Hull family owned most of the land in those parts.

The Harrigans and Fitzgeralds spoke Irish, as did about 90 percent of the people of Cork until the mid-19th century. The oldest children of William and Ann received some schooling in English, however, at the little school at Leamcon near the Harrigan and Fitzgerald farms. As Catholics living on the borderline of the Catholic parishes of Goleen and Schull, they were served by priests of both parishes.

HISTORY OF SCHULL PARISH

What we used to be told of the history of West Cork is probably more fiction than fact. According to legends that modern historians tend to disregard or treat with caution, there were three early invasions of southern Ireland from the continent. First were the Firbolgs, a pastoral people. They were conquered by the warlike De Danaans about 1000 B.C., who, in turn were conquered by the Milesian Celts, probably from Spain, about 500 B.C. Some think the Firbolgs and De Danaans, as well as the Milesians, were of Celtic stock. A good source for sorting out the fiction from the fact is T.F. O'Rahilly, *Early Irish History and Mythology* (1964).

Archaeological evidence indicates that a hunting and fishing society existed earlier than 6000 B.C. Farmers and herdsmen arrived about 3500 B.C. Bronze workers came about 2000 B.C. The rich copper deposits on Mount Gabriel were worked from perhaps as early as 1200 B.C., according to carbon-dating. The copper was mixed with the tin of Cornwall to make bronze. Ships of many lands anchored in Schull harbor to take on cargoes from the mines at Rossbrin. These mines were abandoned in ancient times but were rediscovered and worked for a while in the 19th century.

The Mizen Peninsula was known anciently as Ivagha or *Uí[bh]*

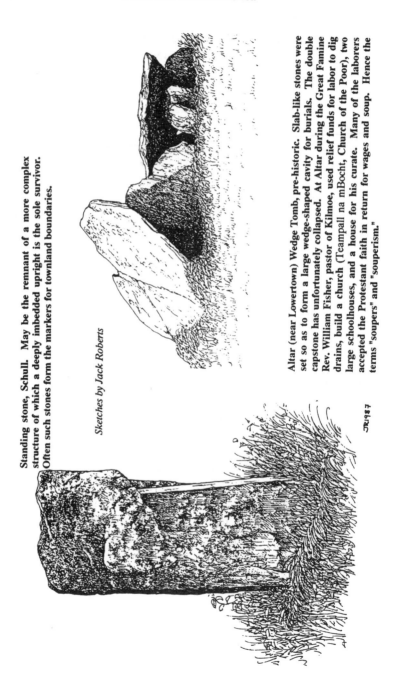

Standing stone, Schull. May be the remnant of a more complex structure of which a deeply imbedded upright is the sole survivor. Often such stones form the markers for townland boundaries.

Sketches by Jack Roberts

Altar (near Lowertown) Wedge Tomb, pre-historic. Slab-like stones were set so as to form a large wedge-shaped cavity for burials. The double capstone has unfortunately collapsed. At Altar during the Great Famine Rev. William Fisher, pastor of Kilmoe, used relief funds for labor to dig drains, build a church (Teampall na mBocht, Church of the Poor), two large schoolhouses, and a house for his curate. Many of the laborers accepted the Protestant faith in return for wages and soup. Hence the terms "soupers" and "souperism."

Knock Tower, near Lowertown and close to the Fitzgerald & Harrigan leasehold in Druinane Townland. Signal towers such as this one were built during the Napoleonic Wars, spaced on the coast twenty miles apart, to give warning of approaching enemy ships. Photo by Lee Snodgrass, 1982.

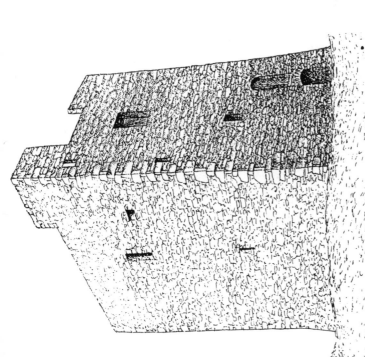

Leamcon or Black Castle at Castlepoint (see cover of this book). Built by the O'Caol branch of the O'Mahoneys about the middle of the 15th century. In 1603, rebel forces finally yielded to Sir George Carew ("Siege of Dunboy"). An instrument called a "Sow" was used in an attempt to undermine the structure, but the castle is still in fine condition. Sketch by Jack Roberts.

Mizen Head, Co. Cork, the extreme southern point of Ireland's mainland. Photo with permission of John Hinde, Ltd., Dublin

Schull Harbor, West Cork, situated on an inlet of Roaring Water Bay. Photo with permission of Cardall Ltd., Dublin.

Eachach, the name of the tribal group of which the O'Mahonys became the leading family, the surname O'Mahony coming into use in the 11th century. The area was also sometimes called *An Fonn Iartharach*, "the western land." Its history was tied to the Ui Eachach or O'Mahonys from the 5th to the 17th centuries, and to other great families such as the O'Driscolls, O'Sullivans, O'Donovans, and the McCarthys (who dominated West Cork).

A succession of twenty O'Mahony chieftains were undisputed rulers of the Mizen from the 12th to the 17th centuries. By 1400 they had built twelve castles ringing the Mizen from Dunbeacon to Rossbrin, including one at Leamcon. Their ships and fighting men exacted a wealth in tolls from fishing vessels from Portugal, Spain, France, the Netherlands, and England. Roaring Water Bay had become one of the richest fishing grounds in Europe. The cosmopolitanism of the coast, especially the Spanish connection, is evidenced by place names such as Spanish Cove, Spanish Point, Galley Cove, and, on the eastern side of the bay near Baltimore, Spanish Island and Spain Tower.

The O'Mahonys and many other Irish chieftains were only imperfectly Christianized; at least that was an argument advanced by Norman King Henry II of England in 1155 to obtain the Pope's permission and blessing to conquer Ireland, which his knights succeeded in doing for him within the two following decades. McCarthy, as king of Desmond (South Munster), submitted to Henry in 1171, while O'Mahony, a minor lord, was not required to submit.

Bloody battles over succession were the rule. In 1232 Donal McCarthy plundered the land of Muircheartach, an O'Mahony chief, and killed his three sons. Not only was there considerable internecine warfare, but the McCarthy and O'Mahony chiefs sometimes took opposite sides and sometimes joined in fighting their Norman and, later, English conquerors.

There is little evidence that the O'Mahonys of this era were members of the church hierarchy (none was ever Bishop of Cork or Ross). However, centuries after the Norman invasion there is some record of O'Mahonys among the religious martyrs: in 1594, Blessed

John Cornelius O'Mahony, a Jesuit, was hanged; in 1642, Father Francis O'Mahony, a Franciscan, was imprisoned, tortured despite his advanced age, and then hanged with his cincture.

There is some evidence, however, for O'Mahony patronage of Gaelic education. Although the McCarthys had been the principal sponsors of the O'Daly family of bards, the O'Mahonys sponsored one branch of the O'Dalys at Kilcrohane. In 1642, Sir William Hull of Leamcon complained that two ploughlands at Kilcrohane that he held on a long lease from the Bishop of Cork had been taken from him by several O'Dalys and others. The ruins of their bardic school can still be seen.

Finin of Rossbrin, an O'Mahony chief, was considered the most learned man of his time in Latin, Irish, and English. Before his death in 1496, Finin had translated into Irish the popular *Travels of Sir John Mandeville*. Finin may have been educated at a local school from which some think the village of Schull derived its name. The parish church was known in Finin's time as Sancta Maria de Schola, and *Scoil Mhuire* is Irish for School of Mary, but Cork historian Diarmuid Ó Murchadha has told this writer that he has found no evidence for this derivation of the village's name. (See Appendix B, Irish Terminology.)

The Elizabethan conquest was first experienced by the O'Mahonys in 1562 when Donal O'Mahony of Rossbrin on the Mizen Peninsula was condemned and hanged in Cork City after being charged with piracy.

Many of the Gaelic chiefs accepted the "surrender and re-grant" proposals of Henry VIII and his daughter Elizabeth I, by which they abandoned the Gaelic system of communal, tribal ownership and swore loyalty to the English crown in return for personal title to all or part of the tribal lands. English Law was thus imposed on Ireland, eclipsing the Gaelic order of things. But outright confiscation of the lands was extensive in the late 1500s, continuing until the 1690s through the Parliamentary and Williamite wars, when the conquest and confiscations were complete. The lands of the O'Mahonys had been reduced considerably by 1622, when Sir William Hull was occupying the O'Mahony castle at Dunmanus. In that year Hull also obtained a lease on the castle and land at Leamcon from representatives of Conor O'Mahony.

Pirates and smugglers found the many little coves and bays safe haven. As late as the first quarter of the 17th century, twenty-five pirate vessels used the cove at Leamcon (Croagh Bay) as their lair. Sir William Hull was occupier of Leamcon Castle and Vice-President of Munster (Vice-Admiral, appointed in 1609, according to one source). In 1616, he contracted with Sir Richard Boyle, who became first Earl of Cork, to engage in the pilchard fishing business in Cork and Waterford. Hull also made profitable arrangements with the most notorious pirates along the coast. By the time of the Parliamentary War in the 1640s, he had substantially increased his holdings over a wide area of West Cork. The holdings included a lease on the town of Crookhaven, which was attacked in December 1641 by 700 rebels under Fionn ("fair-headed") Ó Mahowne of Kilmoe, so Hull reported in a claim submitted on October 22, 1642, for damages incurred. O'Mahony forces were "the firste Robbers," Hull testified, who destroyed some of his houses and his fishing cellars at Crookhaven and attacked the pilchard fish-house at Leamcon Castle, which Hull had built to withstand, he thought, a siege of 4,000 warriors. His family at Leamcon barely escaped with the help of a ship captain he had hired. The captain set fire to the castle, leaving the whole countryside to the rebels.

The rebels carried away about 2,000 barrels of salt from the fish cellars at Leamcon and Dunbeacon, valued at over £600, and other goods also valued at £600, including 1,300 sheep worth £173. Hull further reported that he had an income of £280 a year from rents at Crookhaven town, £280 from lands in Kilmoe and Leamcon, £1,500 to £2,000 from pilchard fishing, and £92 from half the rents at Clonakilty to the east. He counted his yearly losses at £1,150, in addition to £7,500 in property. At Clonakilty, the rebels destroyed his house, carried away the floorboards, and burned the orchards and gardens.

"Dermont Ó Coghlan, Rebell, of Scull" was among those

named by Hull in his 1642 deposition as owing him money "before the troubles," notes Diarmuid Ó Murchadha in *Family Names of County Cork*. Perhaps this was the Dermot or Dermont of Long Island who, with a brother, was outlawed in 1643 for taking part in the rebellion.

Hull received £7,679 in claims. The O'Mahony lands at Leamcon, leased in 1622, now belonged to him and his heirs in "fee simple" forever. These amounted to more than 1,200 acres in and around Leamcon Castle, including the townlands of Derryleary and Drinane, where two hundred years later the Fitzgeralds and Harrigans of this study were paying rents to his descendants.

Also confiscated were the lands of O'Mahony chiefs at Dunmanus (1594 acres), Skeaghanore (1567 acres), Ballyrisode and Durrus (1210 and 646 acres), Coolagh (751 acres), and Kilcrohane (182 acres). Many of the O'Mahonys became tenants on their former lands, the new landowners in time to come bearing names such as Sir Richard Hull, Lord Kingston, and Sir William Petty. It is thought that Finin O'Mahony of Leamcon may have been transplanted to Connacht.

The O'Mahonys of the Mizen made a last, futile effort to reclaim their lands by supporting King James II. For this, sixteen O'Mahonys were outlawed in 1690, and none was ever restored to his patrimony by the Court of Claims.

PENAL CODES

The penal laws of the 17th and 18th centuries were designed to put an end forever to the rebellious behavior of the native Irish. Various codes of marked severity were passed in the two decades following the defeat of the forces under Catholic King James at the Battle of the Boyne in 1690 and the capitulation the following year of Patrick Sarsfield's forces at Limerick. Despite the provisions of the treaty struck with Sarsfield, the English rulers set out to destroy the Catholic Church in Ireland, as the key to the strategy of ending rebellion. All the bishops along with the "regular" clergy, mostly Jesuits, Franciscans, Dominicans, Augustinians, were ordered to leave

Ireland by May 1, 1698. They were subject to charges of high treason and punishment by execution if they dared to return. "Secular" clergy, not members of the orders, were required by law to register, post a substantial bond to cover transportation into exile and other costs in the event they violated any of the penal codes, and take an oath swearing allegiance to a Protestant king forever.

In 1698, 444 priests of an estimated 1,237 were reported to have been transported, mostly to French ports and Lisbon. In that year 12 priests (9 secular, 3 regular), unnamed, were said to be residing in the Baltimore Revenue District. One or more of these presumably served the Mizen Peninsula parishes. In 1700 the parish priest of Kilmoe and West Schull was Tadhg Ó Cochláin (Coghlan). By 1703, only two bishops, both in hiding, remained in Ireland. By 1708, the number had increased to three, one in prison, a second sickly, and a third in hiding. By 1710, only 33 priests of a then-reported total of about 1,100 had taken the Oath. Many of them had even refused to register.

In 1714, a report of priests who allegedly had visited Cork City contained these items: "Daniel Carthy alias Gehy deceased, East Skull" and "Teige Calleghan [same as Tadhg O Cochlain?], Skull and Kilmoo," after whose name was the notation "refused the oath." In 1731, two Mass-houses existed on the Mizen Peninsula, one in Schull and the other in Goleen. In the same year it was reported that for the parish of Kilmoe and surrounds "fryars frequently landed here from France who disperse themselves through the Country."

At the same time illegal traffic in priests was being conducted with the help of smugglers, especially along the rugged coasts of southwest Cork and Kerry. The smuggling trade was in wine and brandy for the wool that the Irish were forbidden by law to export to any country but England. A Protestant bishop complained at this time that "Popish priests were dayly convey'd thro' said parishes [Kilmoe and Schull] into ye inland Country who are landed at ye harbour of Crookhaven....by shipping from France and other countries, which priests, I am credibly informed, are mostly Fryars." On January 9, 1710, William Hull, Justice of the Peace, examined innkeeper Thomas Morgan of Crookhaven. Morgan reported that two years past Thomas Grady had spirited two "fryars" ashore at Coosane near Schull. There they were met by "Kean Mahon of Meenterory" and sheltered by Edmund Hodnett, who provided them with horses and arms before conveying them to Cork City.

ELSEWHERE IN IRELAND

In 1719, the Irish House of Commons approved an elaborate bill against Papists, one clause calling for branding with a red-hot iron the letter "P" on the cheeks of all unregistered priests. The Irish Privy Council changed the penalty to castration before sending the bill to London. There, the ministers restored the branding provision, perhaps because of diplomatic pressure from Catholic France, returning it to Dublin where the Irish Parliament had the power to reject but not amend. The Irish House of Lords, objecting to a clause in the bill concerning leases which Catholics had been allowed to make, rejected the whole bill. Regarding these events, historian W.E.H. Lecky of Trinity College, himself a Protestant, wrote: "It is a memorable fact in the moral history of Europe that as late as 1719 this penalty [castration] was seriously proposed by the responsible government of Ireland."

In 1723, the same House passed a fierce new bill against unregistered priests, providing high bounties for Discoverers ("priest-catchers"). But this was more sound and fury than action, as evidenced by the 1731 *Report on the State of Popery in Ireland*. It is a remarkably valuable document. The returns therein, submitted pursuant to an order of the "Lords Committees," were prepared by local Church of Ireland officials, and they covered every diocese and parish in Ireland. They enumerated the number and location of Mass-houses, private chapels, friaries, nunneries, and popish schools, and the number of Catholic clergy. It is clear from the reports by respondents who had no good reason to exaggerate the Catholic presence (they were supposed to enforce the codes) that the Catholic Church was functioning openly in every diocese and in almost every parish, despite the codes. It was evident, even by 1731, that the codes against the practice of the Catholic religion were a failure. The enforcement, if at all, was usually only token and spasmodic. Father William P. Burke in *The Irish Priests in the Penal Times (1660-1760)* remarks that "upon the whole a steady defervescence of bigotry is noticeable after 1720."

The 1731 report indicated that there were 1,445 secular clergy, 254 regular clergy (including friars), "several" bishops, 9 nunneries, 664 Mass-houses, 54 private chapels, and 549 popish schools, in a population of 1,309,769 Catholics in a total population of 2,010,221.

In 1766 there were 480 friars in Ireland, including 231 Franciscans, 147 Dominicans, 68 Augustinians, and 34 Carmelites. Catholics in some areas felt as harassed by itinerant and poorly educated friars demanding fees for their services as they were by tithe collectors for the Protestant Church of Ireland. In mid-century, the practice of ordaining young, uneducated men to the priesthood before sending them to the continent to study was abandoned on orders from Rome.

The population figures reveal the failure of the codes to win the majority away from the Roman Catholic church. In 1766, Ulster was the only province with a Protestant majority.

1766 POPULATION	CATHOLIC	PROTESTANT
Connacht	246,142	23,718
Leinster	474,863	214,173
Munster	491,738	134,061
Ulster	194,602	379,217
	1,407,345	751,169

The real success of the codes was in the Protestant acquisition of land. Until the Gavel Act was repealed in 1778, the land of a Catholic, upon death, had to be divided among all his sons, unless the oldest son apostatized, a recipe that insured balkanization and impoverishment of estates. Although quite a few Catholic families managed to evade this requirement (some inheritors formally apostatized but secretly remained Catholics), Catholic ownership of land dropped from about 14 percent at the beginning of the 18th century to about 5 percent by the last quarter of the century.

PRIEST-CATCHERS

Priest-catching does not seem to have been a popular or successful pastime in West Cork, nor elsewhere in Ireland. Professional priest-catchers, seeking bounties, were generally held in low esteem even by the authorities. Two of the most notorious, J. Garcia and Edward Tyrrell, came to grief.

Garcia, said to be a Spanish or Portuguese Jew, arrived in Dublin in 1717, converted to Protestantism, and took up the priest-catching profession. Between 1718 and 1720, he received a total of £125 for his services from Dublin authorities. They tired of him by 1722, after he had made a number of self-pitying and unsuccessful appeals for a pension.

More notorious than Garcia was the fallen gentleman Edward Tyrrell, who made several expeditions throughout the countryside in 1712 in search of priests and bounties. In that year he also married. It was soon learned that he had three (or four) other wives. Entrapped, he was tried, confronted with the testimony of his wives, and convicted. Tyrrell was hanged at Newgate on May 23, 1713.

In Limerick, one priest-catcher had these lines cut by his neighbor on the back of his tombstone (as reported by Burke in *Irish Priests in Penal Times*):

> *God is pleased when man doth cease to sin*
> *The devil is pleased when he a soul doth win*
> *Mankind are pleased whene'er a villain dies*
> *Now all are pleased for here Jack Cusack lies.*

Enforcement of the codes against priests and Catholic schoolmasters, especially in the overwhelmingly Catholic countryside, was difficult and even dangerous business. Most magistrates and other Protestant gentry would have none of it and, while lamenting the superstitions of the peasantry, looked the other way. In 1731, for the *Report on the State of Popery,* the mayor of Galway noted that his sheriffs could find no member of the forbidden friars in his town. But the account book of the Augustinian friars has an entry for 1731, reading: "November 9....a bottle of wine for ye sheriffs 1s 1d." The same mayor reported that his sheriffs could find no Dominicans in their reputed friary. Yet an entry in the Dominican account book reads: "For claret to treat ye Sherifs in their search, ye 11th [of the month] 2s 2d."

To be sure, there were occasional outbreaks of enthusiastic enforcement, short-lived. In February, 1744, in a swoop by priest-hunters in Dublin, Father Nicholas English was arrested while saying Mass. Two Dominicans, among others, were caught and arrested. Several months later Viscount Taafe, ambassador to England from Austria, visiting Dublin from whence came his own forebears, found the doors to the St. Stephen's Street Chapel nailed shut by government order. He wrote a letter of complaint to the King of England after being treated badly, he claimed, by Irish government officials.

In 1756, the magistrates of Cork City closed all Catholic chapels and what they called "oratories." They took the keys, after which Catholics armed with fists and clubs tried to open the chapels, attacking armed Protestants who opposed them. There were some injuries to both sides but no fatalities. The chapels were reopened shortly thereafter, but one priest was held in jail for several months.

EXECUTION OF FR. NICHOLAS SHEEHY

Generally, however, clergy were harassed only when they were perceived as a threat to property. This was evident during the violence of the 1760s when the Catholic bishops distanced themselves from the secret Whiteboy organization that opposed both tithes and pasture enclosures. Father Nicholas Sheehy of Clogheen, accused of complicity in a murder allegedly perpetrated by Whiteboys, was executed at Clonmel, County Tipperary, in 1766, a "notorious case of injustice," wrote W.E.H. Lecky. The head of the hanged and quartered priest remained spiked over Clonmel Jail for twenty years, and the priest's grave became a place of pilgrimage. During the last of three trials, a witness named Keating testified that Sheehy was in Keating's house at the time of the murder. Keating was then arrested on suspicion of being a Whiteboy himself.

THE REMARKABLE BISHOP SWEETMAN

Bishops were exercising jurisdiction despite the codes. Quite revealing is the career of Nicholas Sweetman, bishop of Ferns in Wexford from 1745 to 1786. Sweetman was taken under arms and imprisoned briefly in Dublin Castle in 1751, after being charged by a priest whom he had suspended with recruiting soldiers for the Pretender James III. He was released after favorably impressing the Viceroy, Lord Chesterfield, with his urbane good manners, his erudition, and his willingness to cooperate with the authorities. Lord Chesterfield became his lifelong admirer and friend, and Sweetman continued to exercise his ecclesiastical authority, in flagrant violation of the codes. During his long tenure, he had much less trouble from the civil authorities than from priests he considered renegade or incompetent. Sweetman also was distressed by Franciscan friars who disputed his authority over church property and other matters. He ordered them to take down the Stations of the Cross, and he condemned other "superstitions" such as blessing water and sprinkling it on sick people, cattle, and fields. Sweetman called the priests who did this "faery doctors." His battle with the friars raged for twenty years and was carried to the Vatican.

NANO NAGLE, FOUNDER OF THE PRESENTATION SISTERS

Also revealing is the career of Honora "Nano" Nagle, born in Ballygriffin, County Cork, in 1718 of parents in good circumstances. Her father had managed to hold onto his land while still adhering to the Catholic faith. Between 1755 and 1784, Paris-educated Nano Nagle established a number of schools in Cork City, where her brother Joseph had property and commercial interests. She recruited the French order of Ursulines to establish a community in 1771, and later founded the Sisters of the Presentation of the Blessed Virgin Mary, an order devoted exclusively to helping the poor.

Some of the more affluent Catholics in Cork City, who had the most to lose, reviled Nano for spending so much money and energy educating "beggars' brats." Some Protestants were alarmed not only by Nano but by "the multiplication of private places of Catholic worship and the swarms of Jesuits." Nano compromised by forbidding her nuns to wear their habits publicly. Fearing repercussions, she even objected strongly when the Ursulines in 1779 decided to flout the codes by donning their habits.

In the final analysis, enforcement of the penal codes turned out to be impossible in a land with a Catholic population of 90 percent outside of Ulster. With few exceptions, priests and their bishops conducted their business in the last half of the 18th century, and even before, with little effective opposition, as long as they did not confront or inconvenience the landlords or magistrates. Hard and brutal incidents of enforcement of the codes appear to be rather isolated and sporadic events, if viewed over the course of the entire 18th century. Certainly, nothing approaching the persecutions of prior centuries prevailed, in degree of barbarity or in numbers.

MASS ROCKS

By mid-18th century, the posting of sentries at Mass Rocks was usually a thing of the past. The open-air Masses, romanticized in folklore, continued in many parishes. They were, however, "far more a product of poverty than of persecution of religion itself," believes historian Father James Coombes of Skibbereen, who called the author's attention to one Mass Rock in West Cork that could not have been situated in a more vulnerable location.

The open-air Masses were sometimes a consequence of landlords refusing to lease land for a Catholic chapel, or to allow rock-quarrying for its construction, or to permit Mass-houses to remain on land that was being cleared and improved. Even as late as 1781, Lord Doneraile, in a fit of pique, closed every Mass-house on his estate in County Cork. This was after he had been convicted of horsewhipping, kicking, and beating almost to death an 81-year-old parish priest and his housekeeper. Doneraile was furious that he could not get the priest to lift the excommunication of a person living in adultery. The old priest claimed in conscience that he was unable to discuss the matter. The enraged Lord was tried on an assault charge and fined £1,000,

It is easy to argue that the truly grievous crime of colonial rule during the 18th century was not the enforcement of the codes, ugly as they appeared on paper, but rather the physical and cultural impoverishment of an ancient, proud people. Despite all, the Church survived. It can also be argued that the Church, with its priests, was the chief single force that provided some hope and dignity to the degraded and despairing peasantry. That goes a long way toward explaining the respect that the Irish have given their priests right into modern times.

SETBACKS IN CORK

There were some setbacks to the Church in Cork and Schull. In 1773, Father Jeremiah Harte was appointed Parish Priest of Schull. The following year he took the Oath, renouncing the Popish communion at a ceremony at the Cathedral of St. Fin Barre [Finbarr], Cork City. The apostasy earned him a living as a Church of Ireland pastor. Even more disappointing to the Catholics of Schull was the apostasy in 1787 of their bishop, John Butler, in Cork City. He resigned his bishopric when over seventy years of age to marry in a Protestant Church and to be eligible to assume his family's inherited title, Lord Dunboyne. He returned to the Catholic faith in 1800, the year of his death, and left £1,000 to establish a Dunboyne Foundation at the seminary in Maynooth.

THE ASCENDANCY

The whole period of what came to be known as the Protestant Ascendancy was also a dark period for the ruling class. Many Ascendancy families fell into decadence over the course of generations. In 1900, one product of the class, the noted writer Standish James O'Grady, wrote with contempt that the Ascendancy Protestants "had once owned all Ireland from the Centre to the Sea, but now....they are rotting from the land....without having to their credit one brave deed, without one brave word." Dr. Mahaffy of Trinity College, also a member of the Ascendancy, wrote that his class had become "idle, afflicted with boorish ignorance and lacking in public spirit. They neither read books, nor collected libraries and as regards education, they were going backwards – even their women cared for nothing but hunting and racing." But the whole truth over the course of two centuries, as Professor James Donnelly and others have shown, was that many who bore the surnames of these Ascendancy families had themselves fallen into comparative poverty. Some could hardly be distinguished from the native Irish. Even some of the greatest of the landlords were barely clinging to over-mortgaged estates. (See Notes for Chapter 1: *Over-Encumbered Estates.*)

The Protestant Ascendancy was the class of people that were masters of the Mizen Peninsula. Catholics, especially the poor cottiers and laborers, had no practical appeal in the law. Their landlord was often the magistrate. It is not surprising, therefore, that the system of justice merited the cynicism of the masses of Catholics, as expressed in this jingle:

> *The law doth punish man or woman*
> *That stole the goose from the common*
> *But lets the greater felon loose*
> *That stole the common from the goose.*

In Schull parish, circa 1830, as reported in Lewis, *A Topographical Dictionary of Ireland* (1837), a manorial court was held at the Hull castle at Leamcon every third Monday, at which debts under five pounds were recoverable. An ecclesiastical court was held occasionally at "the manor belonging to the Bishop of Ross" (presumably the glebe house occupied by the curate of absentee rector Anthony Traill). Petty sessions were held at Toormore on alternate weeks in matters of grievance.

EDUCATION

Catholic education was proscribed by the penal codes. What education there was for Catholic children, if their parents did not send them to a proselytizing Protestant Charter School (almost none did) was furnished illegally and surreptitiously by the hedge-schools. These flourished from the 1640s, with the death of the Gaelic Bardic schools. The 1731 *Report on the State of Popery* indicates that Catholic hedge schoolmasters were functioning quite openly, if illegally, in many parishes. Little effort, the report indicated, was being made to capture, fine, and imprison them, as the codes demanded. These itinerant scholars were known to give instruction in Greek and Latin as well as in Irish history. There were reports of students illiterate in English who could read Homer in Greek and spout Virgil in Latin.

The codes were relaxed by Acts of 1782 and 1792. Among the *Parliamentary Papers* prepared in the 1820s is a detailed report on the schools. In Schull Parish by 1826, seven of the ten schools were taught by Catholic masters. Historian Father Patrick Hickey gives figures on schoolmasters' stipends and on attendance. They reveal that the poorest Protestant schools were better off than the "best" Catholic schools. The best paid Catholic teacher taught at Schull and received ten pounds a year for a class of forty-two Catholics and two Protestants. The best paid Protestant teachers received 24 pounds at Gubeen for a class of 58 children, including five Catholics, and 25 pounds at Ballydehob for a class of 45 pupils, 4 of them Catholic. The worst paid teacher taught at Leamcon, close by the Fitzgeralds and Harrigans, receiving only two pounds for a class of seventeen Catholics and one Protestant conducted in a structure described as "a miserable little hut." Almost certainly in that squalid structure the Harrigans and Fitzgeralds learned to read and write.

The Catholic schools were supported entirely by subscription of the parents. The religious census taken in 1834 (as reported in the *Parliamentary Gazetteer of Ireland*) revealed that Schull Parish had two Protestant Sunday schools attended by eighty scholars; seven Catholic hedge-schools usually attended in summer by about 243 scholars; and nine other daily schools, two of which (Catholic) "were supported wholly by fees" and attended by 212 boys and 173 girls. Government aid ostensibly came with the advent of a National School System in 1831-32. There was, however, a catch: an application for a National School, even one conducted by Catholics, and a license for the Catholic schoolmaster had to be submitted to the local Church of Ireland rector for his endorsement. In 1836, the Reverend Robert Traill refused to sign an application submitted by the Catholic school at Ballydehob, even though the school was detached from the chapel as required, with no crucifix, statues, or religious pictures in evidence, as also required.

On September 10, 1844, James McCarthy, middleman of Kilmoe/Goleen, reported to the Devon Commission that the landed proprietors of the area persisted in refusing a site of barren rock for a Catholic schoolhouse, "though a hundred acres of it would not be worth a farthing." A request to quarry slate for the local Catholic chapel, McCarthy reported, had also been turned down. In 1838 the Catholic school at Schull achieved National School status. But as late as 1845, two years before he was to succumb to famine fever, Dr. Traill was still protesting.

MORE UNREST

Despite the relaxation of the codes, unrest was the rule. There were bloody encounters at County Wexford and in parts of Ulster during the Rising of 1798, English cannon and muskets against Irish pikes. General John Moore was ordered to abort any rising in southwest Cork, from Skibbereen to the Mizen Head. He assigned Major Nugent to the peninsula itself, from Ballydehob to Ballydevlin. Moore's published diary explained his strategy: "to forage the whole country [and] to treat the people with as much harshness as possible....and to supply [the troops] with whatever provisions were necessary to enable them to live well." Moore's purpose was "to excite terror and by that means to obtain our end speedily." The plan was successful. "The terror was great....the moment a redcoat appeared everybody fled," Moore wrote.

Nugent's five companies, after a three-week campaign, extracted 800 pikes and 3,400 stands of arms "in poor condition." General Moore, who had observed on his way to fight at Wexford that he would be on the side of the rebels if he had been Irish, is well spoken

Mrs. Ellen Lucy.

Oshkosh May Still Claim the Oldest Woman in Wisconsin.

Mrs. Ellen Lucy of this city enjoys the distinction, without doubt, of being the oldest woman in Wisconsin if not in the United States. She was born in Ireland in 1778, and is in her 109th year. Mrs. Lucy lives on Merritt street with her son, Policeman John Lucy, who was born when his mother was fifty four years old, and is the youngest of ten children, four of whom are now living. Mrs. Lucy came to America in 1851 and settled with her husband in the state of Maine. Four years ago she came west to live with her son, and although then past her 104th year made the journey alone. Having some doubts about his mother's age, which were also entertained by other members of the family, Mr. Lucy wrote to a married sister with whom Mrs. Lucy had lived before coming to this city, for data regarding her birth. His sister immediately wrote to the parish priest in the county of Cork, Ireland, in which Mrs. Lucy first saw the light, and as the law with regard to the registration of births and marriages is very rigid, there was no difficulty in determining the dates, and Mrs. Lucy's statement that she had passed her 105th year proved to be true. These facts were obtained soon after Mrs. Lucy came here. One of the coldest days this winter, she made up her mind to go out calling, and the family could not deter her from her purpose. Mr. Lucy luckily happened along just as she was emerging from the house and was obliged to put his foot down quite determinedly before the old lady would give up. Mrs. Lucy is quite talkative when once started, and if she isn't checked will become quite noisy, talking as fast and as earnestly as a lecturer. Her eyes, which retain much of the brightness of youth, flash and sparkle when she is relating some of the scenes of her youth. Her memory as to the events of the present day is not retentive. It is said she doesn't have much recollection of the affairs of yesterday, but can relate and repeat very many things she learned in her youth. She can give no facts of history nor relate any events of stirring interest. The only bit of interesting history that has been obtained from her is that during the rebellion in Ireland in 1798, her family, Mrs. Lucy being then nineteen, was obliged to hide themselves in a cave. She claims to have been married at twenty two. From her son it was learned that Mrs. Lucy goes to bed regularly at eight o'clock and is up or awake at six. She sleeps and eats well, has not been sick since she came west, and has no disease of any kind. *Oshkosh Weekly Northwestern, Jan. 19, 1887.*

Ellen Harrigan Lucey in 1889, age 111, but see Appendix D: "Oldest Woman in Wisconsin," p. 106. She recalled hiding in a cave during the sweep of the Mizen Peninsula by British troops in 1798. Oshkosh Museum photo.

of by some Irish historians. His use of "terror" was designed to eliminate bloodshed. There was no rising, no bloodshed, on the peninsula. Ellen Harrigan, who married Tim Lucey and who lived to be 112 (but see Appendix D), was nineteen years of age at the time of Major Nugent's sweep. Her recollections were reported ninety years later, in the January 19, 1887, *Oshkosh [Wisconsin] Daily Northwestern*. She told the reporter that her family "was obliged to hide in a cave."

Relations between Catholics and Protestants seem to have improved somewhat in the first quarter of the 19th century. The Catholics maintained a small chapel in Ballinskea (now part of Arderawinny) townland near Lowertown. It was the closest chapel to the Fitzgeralds and Harrigans. It is quite possible that members of the family were present when the roof collapsed during a celebration of Mass on April 27, 1825. Landlord Richard Edward Hull and Church of Ireland rector Reverend Anthony Traill (father of Robert Traill, referred to earlier) helped Father Michael Prior, Parish Priest of Goleen, to raise subscriptions for a new chapel. Hull donated twenty guineas, a rent-free lease of the site, and permission to quarry rocks and bog-oak for the construction. Traill, "who was always kindly disposed toward his Catholic neighbors," according to one local historian who cited the fact that Traill had forgiven the tithes during the famine of 1822, donated thirty guineas, equivalent of thirty-one pounds ten shillings. He was, however, an absentee rector whose real neighbors were in County Antrim, as we shall see.

The religious devotion of the Catholics was reported by a Protestant gentleman in a Cork newspaper on December 12, 1825. Describing himself as a "liberal Protestant of Skibbereen," he told how he had ridden in the rain to witness for himself the privations of the Catholics of West Schull and to observe the first Mass said on the Hull-donated site. "I saw from the public road at least 2,000 men and women kneeling on the side of a barren mountain, assisting in silence and in apparent reverence at the ceremony of the Mass, literally no canopy over them but the broad expanse of the heavens, whilst a heavy winter's shower descended on their uncovered heads."

Among the 2,000, very likely, were the Harrigans, Fitzgeralds, Luceys, *et al.*

The same Cork newspaper reported on June 21, 1826, that "a commodious and stately temple" for the Catholics of Schull was nearing completion. This particularly soft period in Catholic/ Protestant relations was commemorated in a plaque placed in the chapel:

> *To the Glory of*
> *God this chapel was*
> *Erected by Protestants and*
> *Roman Catholics*
> *Founded A.D. 1826*

Almost one hundred years later, in 1919 during the War of Independence, the plaque was smashed into three pieces. Some think that it was a deliberate act of Father T. O'Sullivan, Parish Priest. Others think the stone was broken by accident when the church was being renovated. For a time the pieces were deposited against the back door of the chapel. They were later removed to the parish house at Goleen, with intention to eventually set them in cement for placement in the Lowertown Chapel.

PAYING TITHES

The major grievance of Catholics remained the hated tithe, assessed on Protestant and Catholic alike for the support of the Protestant Church of Ireland. Ironically, even Catholic priests and dissenting Presbyterian, Methodist and other ministers had to pay the tithe. In Schull Parish, according to the religious census taken in 1834, there were 13,912 Catholics in a total parish population of 15,810. Regular Sunday church attendance was only 160 and 130 at the Church of Ireland services at Schull and Ballydehob, with another 240 at three schoolhouses which also served as places of worship. The Wesleyan meeting house had an attendance of 70. The Catholic chapels at Schull and Ballydehob had attendance of 900 and 1700 respectively, with another 950 at the chapel near Lowertown, the one probably attended by the Fitzgeralds and Harrigans.

Until 1823, the tithe each occupier of land had to pay was determined more or less arbitrarily by the authorities. It could amount to as much as ten shillings a year per Irish acre for wheat and potatoes and eight shillings for oats. All pasture land was excluded, thus placing almost the entire burden of the tithe on the Catholic small tillers. By the reform acts of 1823 and 1824, the amount of tithe was fixed at 10 percent of the average price of a barrel of wheat for the seven-year period 1815 through 1821. The price of a barrel was eighteen shillings and six pence a barrel. For Schull and a few other parishes the rate was set at 7 percent, perhaps because of the poor quality and scarcity of tillage land.

The recipient of the substantial tithes for Schull in 1828, the first year under the new system, was the Reverend Anthony Traill, rector. He was the son of Reverend Robert Traill and Jean Dow; was married to the daughter of William Watts-Gayer, Clerk of the Irish House of Lords; and was a nephew of James Traill, bishop of Down and Connor in Ulster. He was also the father of the Reverend Robert Traill who was to succeed him as pastor at Schull. Anthony was an absentee rector, residing in County Antrim where he also held the title of Archdeacon of Connor from 1782 until his death in 1831. He assumed the rectorship of Schull in 1794. That it was a very valuable sinecure is certified by his bishop's testimony, in 1801, that the value of the benefice was £600 per annum. By contract signed on October 25, 1826, by "Richard Edward Hull, Chairman, Special Vestry," and by the two appointed tithe commissioners, Vicar John A. Jagoe (appointed by Traill) and Thomas Evans of Aghadown (appointed by Hull), the absentee rector was guaranteed "850 [pounds] by the year....for the space of 21 years from the first day of November [1826] and shall not be liable to any change or variation in consequence of any change or variation in the price of grain during said period." This was a most generous agreement. It was immune from the drastic and continuing fall in grain prices in the decades following the Battle of Waterloo and the Peace of 1815. Irish produce, so vital to England during the Napoleonic Wars, was no longer in as much demand in English markets.

Traill's perquisites also included use of the glebe house and income from sixty-three acres of land around it, from which an additional £100 income could be derived. Further, in 1829, he received £650 from the Board of First Fruits of the Established Church for construction of the chapel at Ballydehob. Later, he got £208 from the Ecclesiastical Commission for repairs to the Schull church. Traill paid the salaries of two curates. In 1829, they were Reverend John Triphook, who received £80 per annum, and Reverend Alleyn Evanson, who occupied the glebe house and sixty-three acres, from which he derived, according to his own testimony, £100 per annum. The absentee rector also had to pay an undetermined but no doubt substantial sum to his tithe collectors. It has not been determined how much, if any, of the tithes he shared with his superiors (the "living [was] under the alternate patronage of the Crown and the Bishop"), but such sharing was the exception, not the rule. It was said that he contributed to the support of five schools. His son Robert, who succeeded him, was contributing sums of five, ten, and twenty-five pounds to the support of three schools in 1834.

Without any doubt, the Reverend Traill had a magnificent sinecure. So did his curates, especially Reverend Evanson, occupant of the glebe house. This residence was described eloquently and poetically by a contemporary observer, writing for the *Parliamentary Gazetteer of Ireland.* It was "an ancient mansion sheltered down on the shore, in a sunny nook, half-way between the church and the village...under the guardianship of a protecting hill, and some old sycamores in solitary magnificence and unpruned luxuriance, their long branches sweeping the lawn [seeming] to say we are here to show that no one should be [as] comfortable as a good minister." Continuing in this spirit, and without a suggestion of irony, the writer spoke of the parish church itself "on a high elevation over the sea" blending into "a tranquil and blessed scene [harmonizing] with that peace which religious worship communicates and which worldliness with all its pretences and promises cannot give, and cannot take away."

Nevertheless, the world was in fact hinting at taking away some of this blessed peace and privilege. The Earl of Mountcashel, fifty miles away, attacked the privileges of his own church in a letter to the *Cork Constitution* (November 24, 1829), citing as a notorious example the "lucrative parish" of Schull which, he said, had not been visited by its rector, Anthony Traill, for many years. Even more disturbed, no doubt, was Father Mahony, Catholic parish priest of Schull, who was forced to pay twelve shillings and six pence in tithes on eight acres of land. Just as disturbed, surely, were the Harrigans and Fitzgeralds. Daniel Harrigan and James Fitzgerald, listed occupiers of 22 acres in Drinane Mor townland valued at £14.1s., were assessed 19s.7d. in tithes. Edward Holland, George Kingston, and Michael Harrigan of Drinane Beg, occupying 24 acres valued at £16.1s., were assessed £1.2s.6d. Daniel Sullivan and Tim Harrigan of Derryleary (facing Harrigan's Rocks), occupying 36 acres valued at £37.10s., were assessed £2.12s.5d. At 12 pence to the shilling and 20 shillings to the pound, and figuring a laborer's wages at 8 pence per day (if he were fortunate), the tithes on the occupiers of just these three farms represented 141 days of labor per year. These occupiers were paying for the support of a church to which they did not belong, and which they generally abhorred.

RUNDALE

It should be noted that the acreages of listed occupiers are misleading. Most of the farms were jointly owned, the words "and partners" frequently following the names enumerated on the Tithe Applotments for Schull in 1827, suggesting that a form of the ancient Irish system of "rundale" was still practiced in southwest Cork, as it was in many other areas of rural Ireland well into the 19th century. (See Appendix C: Rundale in West Cork.)

A more revealing picture of the holdings of the individual occupiers is provided in the responses to the *Poor Inquiry*.

THE POOR INQUIRY

The wretched condition of the masses is underscored in a remarkable document which historians usually refer to as the *Poor Inquiry*, the product of a British Parliamentary Commission. In 1833, the Commission addressed several score of questions to one or more persons, usually clergymen or magistrates, in each parish in Ireland. For Schull Parish, the respondents were Reverend Robert Traill, who had succeeded his father in 1830, and Father James Barry, Catholic Parish Priest of Schull. For neighboring Kilmoe/Goleen, the respondents were magistrates Richard Notter and Lionel Fleming. They all confirmed the appalling poverty. Most of the tenants in Schull were "more properly labourers holding but small lots." Very few occupiers held as many as three gneeves, the amount of land required for grazing about twenty-four cows, reported Father Barry. One-eighth of a gneeve, grazing for one cow, was the usual, with many occupiers being "third or fourth from the head landlord." About two-thirds of the land was held under middlemen, about one-third under head landlords who were "usually absentee." The average annual rental for a gneeve was nine pounds. An acre of scarce first-quality land rented for 18s.6d, while the poorest land went for 1s.6d. A cabin and kitchen garden rented for two pounds annually, which amounted to the labor of sixty working days. Part or all of the rental frequently was in the form of labor at the six to ten pence per day prevailing rates.

Unemployment was usual. An adult male could earn four to nine pounds per year. His wife and four children might earn an additional seven or eight pounds as beggars, traveling far into the interior of the country while the father was working his potato patch. Such begging was common, the respondents reported.

An adult working male required seven pounds of potatoes daily (his sole diet, supplemented perhaps with a little milk) to be above the starvation line. Thirty-five pounds of "lumpers" were required for a family of six, two adults and four children. This meant that the six-ton annual production of potatoes on a one-acre plot, a quite usual holding, was consumed totally by this family. Nothing was left over to pay the middleman on Gale Day, the twice-yearly moment of reckoning, except the pig that, perhaps, had been fattened enough with lumpers which the family denied themselves. Hence the stories and the jokes about the pig being part of the Irish family, sharing the interior of the cabin. He was certainly an important family member, a bulwark against eviction.

The usual dwelling in Schull Parish, as elsewhere in Ireland, was a windowless hovel of stone and mud. Very few dwellers had straw for bedding, "heath grass or mountain grass being the substitute." Their clothing was "wretched, perhaps one in six [having] clothing to appear at a house of worship on Sundays," reported Father Barry.

A FRENCH OBSERVER

Confirming the Poor Inquiry were the reports of a number of travelers from the Continent, including Gustave de Beaumont, who visited Ireland in the 1830s:

Misery, naked and famishing, that misery which is vagrant, idle, and mendicant covers the entire country; it shows itself everywhere, and at every hour of the day; it is the first thing you see when you land on the Irish coast, and from that moment it ceases not to be present to your view.

The French traveller went on to describe a cabin, one typically used by both farmers and laborers:

Imagine four walls of dried mud (which the rain, as it falls, easily restores to its primitive condition), having for its roof a little straw or some sods, for its chimney a hole cut in the roof, or very frequently the door through which alone the smoke finds an issue. One single apartment contains father, mother, children and sometimes a grandfather or a grandmother; there is no furniture in this wretched hovel; a single bed of straw serves the entire family. Five or six half-naked children may be seen crouched near a miserable fire, the ashes of which cover a few potatoes, the sole nourishment of the family. In the midst of all lies a dirty pig, the only thriving inhabitant of the place, for he lives in filth. The presence of the pig in an Irish hovel may at first seem an indication of misery; on the contrary, it is a sign of comparative comfort. Indigence is still more extreme in the hovel where no pig is to be found.

This dwelling is very miserable, still it is not that of the pauper properly so called. I have just described the dwelling of the Irish farmer or agricultural labourer.

(One looks in vain for such vivid descriptions of the condition of the Irish masses in latter-day "revisionist" history, now much in vogue. For example, nowhere in the 866 pages of R.F. Foster's masterful study *Modern Ireland 1600-1972* is the reader given a look into an Irish cabin, but he will learn much about the nobles and the midling gentry, and the Georgian architecture of Dublin.)

ANTI-TITHE AGITATION IN SCHULL

The general misery was exacerbated by a severe failure of the potato crop and a cholera epidemic in 1831. Reverend Robert Traill was not nearly as "kindly disposed" to the plight of the Catholics as his father, Anthony, had been. He reported to the Parliamentary Commission conducting the *Poor Inquiry* that, in 1832, "the priests and demagogues excited the most alarming disturbances, which yielded alone to military force." Among the demagogues he had in mind, as we shall see, was surely Father James Barry of Schull. Nevertheless, Barry (perhaps with tongue in cheek) reported that "I have never seen or heard of any place more peaceable than this since 1830; in tithe agitation even, there were no outrages worth remark, and none of any other nature that must not be borne with at all times." The events that seemed significant to Traill are described by Desmond Bowen (*The Protestant Crusade in Ireland, 1800-70*) and others. They were two gigantic anti-tithe meetings. At the first, on June 21, 1832, Father Barry himself was reported as leading his "athletic mountaineers" from Schull Parish, joining a crowd of 20,000 at Bantry. Tradesmen marched in procession, each trade having its own banner. The banner of the tailors displayed a picture of James Doyle, Bishop of Kildare and Leighlin, with the inscription, "May our hatred of Tithes be as lasting as our love of justice." A picture of Daniel O'Connell, the great leader from Kerry, was on the other side.

At the second meeting, in July 1832, at the foot of Mount Gabriel in Father Barry's own bailiwick, there was an even greater gathering. On a wet day, boats galore from Cape Clear and Carbery's Hundred Isles in Roaring Water Bay arrived in Schull Harbor, with "streamers flapping in the breeze." The surrounding country-side was festooned "with wreaths and garlands." There were fiddlers, bagpipes and drums. Many Protestant dissenters, Methodists and others who also resented the tithes, were in attendance. It is possi-ble that among those present were some of the direct ancestors of President John Fitzgerald Kennedy whose maternal Fitzgeralds, ac-cording to the Irish Genealogical Office, farmed near Skibbereen (although some say Limerick).

Another priest "demagogue" in prominent attendance at both meetings was Father Thomas Barry, Parish Priest of Bantry, alleged author of some popular satirical verses, quoted here in part:

> *There was a parson who loved 'divershun'*
> *And ne'er was harsh on his flock so few;*
> *'Twas he dressed sleekly, and looked so*
>   *meekly*
> *When preaching weekly to one or two.*
> *They saw him one day and that was Sunday*
> *For early Monday he was off for fun,*
> *To a steeple chase – a hunt or race,*
> *Or else a blaze with a double gun.*
> *The tithe was heavy that he did levy....*
> *This reverend Tory, so runs the story,*
> *Lived in his glory 'til twenty-nine*
> *When 'emancipation' impaired his reason*
> *Which he swore 'twas treason*
> *For the King to sign....*

The short, relatively peaceful period of Catholic/Protestant relations was definitely over. This was underscored not only by the anti-tithe agitation but by the attitude of Reverend Robert Traill who refused in 1836 to approve the application for National School status of the Catholic school at Ballydehob.

THE GREAT FAMINE

All this was on the eve of the Great Famine when, according to the Relief Committee, 4,476 people died of "fever, dysentery, and destitution" in Schull and Kilmoe/Goleen parishes during one twelve-month period, September 1, 1846, to September 12, 1847. (The population of these two parishes, according to the 1841 census, was 24,548.) Only 352 had the means and the energy to emigrate during the same period. Research indicates that the poorer the parish the higher the mortality, and the higher the mortality the lower the emigration rate.

The Famine began with a partial but severe failure of the potato crop in the late summer and early fall of 1845, a consequence of the blight *phytophthora infestans*, for which no cause nor cure was known. The crop totally failed all over Ireland in 1846. The worst year of what English writers called "the distress" and the Irish "Black 47" was 1847 when corpses lay in the hovels and even on the streets of Schull and Skibbereen, their neighbors too weak to remove them for burial. An Englishman who came ashore at Schull in February of 1847 gave this ghastly report:

....we proceeded to East Skull [Ballydehob] on quitting Shirkin. Inland we passed a crowd of 500 people half naked and starving. They were waiting for soup to be distributed amongst them. They were pointed out to us, and as I stood looking with pity and wonder at so miserable a scene, my conductor, a gentleman residing at East Skull, and a medical man, said to me: 'Not a single one of those you now see will be alive in three weeks; it is impossible.' The deaths here average 40 to 50 daily, 20 bodies were buried this morning, and they were fortunate in getting buried at all. The people build [*sic*] themselves up in their cabins, so that they may die together with their children and not be seen by passers-by. Fever, dysentery, and starvation stare you in the face everywhere – children of 10 and 9 years old I have mistaken for decrepit old women, their faces wrinkled, their bodies bent and distorted with pain, the eyes looking like those of a corpse. Babes are found lifeless, lying on their mothers' bosoms. I will tell you one thing which struck me as peculiarly horrible; a dead woman was found lying on the road with a dead infant on her breast, the child having bitten the nipple of the mother's breast right through in trying to derive nourishment from the wretched body. Dogs feed on the half-buried dead, and rats are commonly known to tear people to pieces, who, though still alive, are too weak to cry out. I went into one of the only shops in the place to try and

February 1847 sketches by James Mahoney for the *London Illustrated News*.
TOP: Skibbereen; BOTTOM: Schull, looking toward the west, Ardmanagh
House in background (adaptation by Jack Roberts).

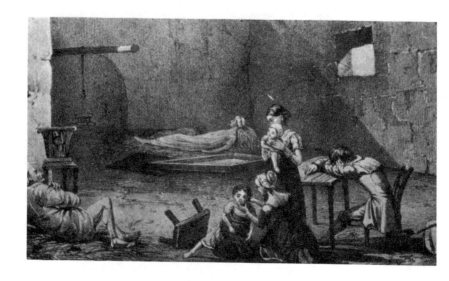

Scenes of starvation and death, Mizen Peninsula, 1847
Sketches by James Mahoney for the *Illustrated London News*

SAMPLING OF TOWNLANDS SCHULL PARISH	AREA + A R P	HOUSES 1841	1851	1861	1871 TOTAL	1871 INHABITED	1871 UNINHAB	*	POPULATION 1841	1851	1861	1871 PERSONS	1871 MALES	1871 FEMALE	VALUATION OF HOUSES & LAND IN 1871 £ s d
Derryleary Townland	183 1 9	34	14	15	13	13	0	5	192	73	78	62	26	36	£67 15s 0d
Drinane "	156 1 21	16	12	6	5	5	0	5	94	60	41	35	15	20	£43 10 0
Dromkeal "	171 0 24	16	10	5	4	4	0	3	94	39	27	22	12	16	£50 0 0
Barnatonicane "	261 2 30	20	6	8	7	7	0	16	128	34	34	41	22	19	£61 10 0
Ballyvonane "	235 0 3	13	6	4	6	6	0	6	82	37	29	28	14	14	£30 10 0
Knockeens "	225 2 6	19	12	9	9	8	1	9	123	81	53	47	25	22	£52 3 0
Leamcon "	136 1 18	12	7	4	2	1	0	6	82	33	30	5	3	2	£92 15 0
Ratooragh "	1,183 2 1	65	29	28	28	26	2	49	381	163	174	157	70	87	£177 15 0
Croagh "	167 3 30	35	14	13	8	8	0	8	187	89	60	42	21	21	£94 10 0
Dunbeacon "	1,459 0 32	142	65	48	50	48	2	46	651	343	260	258	133	125	£424 15 0
Lowertown "	431 3 2	62	29	31	25	24	1	22	342	171	149	132	62	70	£183 15 0
Long Island	341 2 5	61	51	45	41	41	0	31	336	305	254	220	119	101	£134 10 0
Ballydehob Town	20	128	111	103	115	114	1	56	636	589	648	540	313	327	·
Schull Town	34	104	90	110	109	100	5	32	452	535	561	555	262	293	·
TOTAL OF PARISH 98 townlands, 7 inhabited islands, & towns of Ballydehob & Schull	37,922 3 27	3,011	1,747	1,647	1,594	1,559	25	1,655	17,314	11,000	8,950	8,823	4,342	4,481	9,343 13 0

inhabited
uninhabited

* out-offices & farm bldgs.
+ acres, roods, perches
(4 roods = 1 acre, 40 perches = 1 rood)

POPULATION - SCHULL PARISH TOWNLANDS (1841-1871)

Data from 1871 Census of Ireland provided by Tim Cadogan of Cork County Library. Listed are the townlands of the Fitzgeralds, Harrigans, Luceys, Sauntrys of this study, and several neighboring townlands.

get some bread to give away. I was obliged to leave immediately, for I could not stand the stench. On looking again, I discovered the reason – one body lay stretched on a door. And I saw the outline of a form, although covered with a heap of rags, I perceived was also dead. Instead of following us, beggars throw themselves on their knees before us, holding up their dead infants to our sight. (*The Times,* quoted in *Cork Constitution,* March 11, 1847)

The mortality rate for the parish of Schull was one hundred a week during the winter of 1846-47. The effect of the famine on the population of the townlands was catastrophic. Between 1841 and 1871, the population of Derryleary dropped from 192 to 62; of Drinane, from 94 to 35; of Leamcon, from 82 to only 5; of Lowertown, from 342 to 132. The total parish population in 98 townlands, 7 inhabited islands, and the towns of Ballydehob and Schull dropped from 17,314 to 8,823.

In all thirty-two counties of Ireland between 1841 and 1871, the emigrants numbered about three million. By 1891, another 1.1 million emigrated. By that year, 39 percent of all Irish-born persons were living outside of Ireland.

This tragic period in Irish history is called a "hunger," not a "famine," by Cecil (née Fitzgerald) Woodham-Smith in her classic study, *The Great Hunger.* During the worst years, 1846-48, exports from Cork of cattle and butter actually increased substantially, and production of grain, increasingly used for cattle feed, also rose dramatically. It has been estimated that Irish food production was more than sufficient to feed the native population.

Ironically, at the height of the famine in early 1847, miller J.H. Swanton reported that he had 100 to 200 tons of Indian meal (from America) and other flour. He could not dispose of it at his price because the Skibbereen Relief Committee was selling meal "*indiscriminately* for as little as 2s. 2d. a stone." Swanton appealed to the government to buy his horde and therefore save him "the freight of shipping it to another market"! Thus there was food amidst appalling starvation.

RELIGIOUS FEUDING AMIDST FAMINE

Strange as it seems, amidst this "distress," the Protestant and Catholic pastors in West Schull and Goleen became embroiled in bitter religious controversy. In West Schull, the secretary of the Relief Committee was the local Protestant rector of Kilmoe/Goleen since 1842, Reverend William A. Fisher, who would one day become landlord of Toormore, Gorttyowen, and Lissacaha. In February 1847, he was accused by Father Laurence O'Sullivan and his curate Father Thomas Barrett of using famine relief funds to influence starving Catholics to become Protestant. The two priests refused to hand over subscriptions to Fisher and quit the committee. Father O'Sullivan, afflicted with fever himself, journeyed to Cork City in February to raise funds personally. He explained his reasons in a letter published in the *Cork Examiner* on February 8, 1847, written from St. Vincent's Seminary.

Meanwhile, the Reverend Fisher, an Irish speaker, was successfully recruiting a significant number of Catholics (over six hundred by the end of the famine) to his chapel of ease called *Teampall na mBocht* (Church of the Poor) at Altar between Schull and Goleen. Services were in Irish. Historian W.M. Brady, a Protestant who later converted to Catholicism, reported that "the money sent to Mr. Fisher for the relief of the destitute, instead of being distributed in alms gratuitously, was employed in giving labour, and procuring materials to erect this church" *(Clerical and Parochial Records of Cork, Cloyne and Ross,* 1863, vol. 1, p. 176). The converts became known as "soupers," ones who would trade their faith for a bowl of soup. Many of them returned to Father O'Sullivan's church after a mission of six Vincentian priests, including Father John Murphy, who had been successful at winning back soupers at Dingle, arrived in Goleen in the summer of 1848 to help re-convert Fisher's soupers.

Ironically, Father O'Sullivan was later accused by Protestants and some former Catholics of deserting his flock in time of need. They argued that the Catholics turned to Fisher in the absence of their own parish priest. This view has been offered by Peter Somerville-Large in *The Coast of West Cork* ; by Reverend Desmond

Bowen, an ordained Anglican minister, in *The Protestant Crusade in Ireland: 1800-1870*; by Eoghan Harris in his play *Souper Sullivan*; and by a BBC television documentary.

The charge has been answered by historian and priest Father Patrick Hickey, writing in *The Fold* (April 1986) and elsewhere. He points out that the critics of O'Sullivan base their conclusion on local Protestant folklore and on the absence of records of baptism from February to May. They ignore the fact, Hickey argues, that the absence of records does not necessarily mean the absence of a priest. At nearby Aughadown Parish, Father Troy noted in the marriage book, "A frightful famine and fever year, alas, a hundred dying weekly, no marriages or baptisms." Also ignored is that the Goleen curate, Father Barrett, is cited in a number of documents for his charitable activities in 1847. Regarding Bowen's claim that, while the Reverend Fisher himself was ill with fever, the Catholics "quarreled with their priest who fled the community, leaving them without the paternalistic direction he had once given them," Hickey asked Bowen if he could produce any "proper source" for the statement. "He could not," Hickey says, "because it is false."

The facts of record indicate that Father O'Sullivan's absence from the parish was brief. On February 17, the chairman of the Relief Committee, Protestant Richard Notter of Rock Island near Crookhaven, expressed appreciation to O'Sullivan and his curate Thomas Barrett for bringing food to the starving people. The name of Father O'Sullivan is often cited on subscription lists for February through April, after he had obtained substantial donations from Archbishop Murray of Dublin and others. The Goleen church register indicates that O'Sullivan officiated at two marriages on March 16, and he may have returned even before that.

The Reverend Bowen accepts the myth, based entirely (so it seems from his notes) on the memoirs of members of the Irish Church Missions and other Protestants writing twenty to fifty years after the Famine, that Fisher had no choice but to step into the breach and take care of the poor souls deserted by their fearful priest who fled from them in time of starvation and pestilence.

It is more likely, according to this writer's view of the evidence, that Fisher, an unselfish man, wanted to help all people, Protestant and Catholic – spiritually as well as physically. He therefore placed a very high priority on conversions. In an age of Protestant Evangelism in Ireland, Fisher saw conversions from the Popish church as an important part of his ministry. That is why he studied and mastered the Irish language before he arrived on the Mizen Peninsula in 1842. But he was singularly unsuccessful in proselytizing until the Famine, when he acquired converts quickly, only to lose them almost as quickly after the starvation abated.

Many present-day Catholics of the Mizen, with long historical memories, think of Fisher as simply a zealous opportunist. They recall that he did indeed use famine relief funds for digging drains on his own property, building his church and two large schoolhouses and a house for his curate, with the labor of Catholics, many of whom accepted the Protestant faith in return for wages and soup. They think he acted eagerly, unfairly, and selfishly. This view involves no small amount of hindsight and falls short of understanding the complexity of motives, noble and selfish, that drive all human beings.

Myths, however, are always more interesting and dramatic than the facts. The truth about Fisher probably lies somewhere outside the myth accepted by the Reverend Bowen and others on the one hand, and the myth embraced by many Catholics of the Mizen on the other hand. In any case myths, once firmly established, are almost impossible to destroy.

The focus on the Fisher myth can do a great injustice if one ignores the Protestant gentry and their clergy who worked heroically to alleviate the misery of both Catholics and Protestants. Among them was the Reverend Traill. He and family members, including two daughters, worked tirelessly to feed and comfort the starving. Traill himself died of famine fever on April 21, 1847 and was buried at Schull.

Landlord Thomas Swanton of Cranlaith near Ballydehob was so incensed at government foot-dragging that he announced his conversion to repeal of the Act of Union with England. "Murder is going on," he wrote angrily, "for the benefit of Manchester and Liverpool."

Perhaps the greatest heroes of the Famine in West Cork were Frederick F. Trench, Protestant clergyman of County Tipperary, and his cousin Reverend Richard C. Trench, Professor of Divinity at Trinity College in Dublin. Arriving as volunteers on the peninsula in early 1847, they proceeded to organize assistance under the Soup Kitchen Act, working amicably with such clergymen as Father James Barry of Schull and his curate Father John Barry of Ballydehob. James Barry had high praise for the work of the Trenches who quickly set up at least nine eating-houses for soup and meal, feeding 500 a day at each house. By April 1847 the tide of famine and fever began to abate in Schull Parish, and shortly thereafter in Kilmoe/Goleen.

A DIGRESSION

This chapter focuses strongly on political and religious tensions, Protestant and Catholic rivalries, the English versus the Irish, the rich against the poor. The peril of this focus is the inevitability of distortion. The paradigm of class struggle against "800 years of British mis-rule and oppression" is useful, but it has its limits, as "revisionist" historians have rightly pointed out. When pushed too far, it turns people into papier-mâché characters, lacking the flesh and blood of total human beings. Irish men and women were not solely political and religious creatures. Nor were all Catholics poor, even during the worst years of famine and oppression. Nor were all Protestants, including government officials, without the milk of human kindness and the desire for reform.

Even in the 18th century, Catholic merchants in cities such as Cork and Dublin were amassing considerable fortunes in the provisions business and in other occupations. In rural Ireland, middlemen, strong tenants, and even the hated tithe proctors were frequently Catholic. Some old Catholic families managed to hold onto their estates through the centuries of oppression and confiscation.

Joy and laughter, amidst the poverty and misery, were evident. There was dancing to the fiddle and the pipes at the crossroads on summer evenings, and story-telling by the local *seanchaí* at a fireplace on winter evenings. There was feasting at weddings and at wakes. There were local fairs where the small farmer sold his pig, where he enjoyed the musicians and the ballad singers, and where he saw boxing and wrestling matches and other sporting events. There was the infamous faction fighting at these fairs among rival bands of young men from different parishes.

Irish poets were still practicing their ancient art and held in high esteem. The blind poet Carolan, who traveled about Connacht most of his life and is said to have been the greatest and last of the old Irish bards, died in 1737. But a few great ones followed him. The most famous were Eoghan Rua Ó Súilleabháin, born in County Kerry about 1750; Blind Raftery of County Mayo; and Piaras MacGerailt (Pierce Fitzgerald) of County Cork, considered the chief poet of Munster before his death in 1791 at the age of 91.

But probably the most popular poet of all in Cork and elsewhere was Brian Merriman, born about 1749 at Ennystymon, County Clare, in the west of Ireland. He grew up in the village of Feakle where he was educated by hedge schoolmasters. In *The Midnight Court (Cúirt an Mheán-Oíche)*, a poem written about 1780 and consisting of over a thousand lines of rhyming Gaelic verse, Merriman celebrates the rights of women to sex and marriage and satirizes single men, impotent old suitors, and older women married to young men. One caustic passage attacks the conduct of the administration of justice by the British ruling class.

The Midnight Court is a bawdy, good-humored poem that many an Irishman of Merriman's day could spout by heart in its entirety. One character in the poem, an elderly man tricked by his young bride, has this to say (in a liberal translation by Frank O'Connor, who uses rhyming couplets to suggest the assonantal, stressed-syllable rhyming couplets of the original):

> *And I smiled and I nodded and off I tripped*
> *Til my wedding night when I saw her stripped*

And knew too late that this was no libel
Spread in the pub by a jealous rival
By God, 'twas a fact well-supported
I was a father before I started!

A major achievement of Merriman, who died in Limerick in 1805, was to remind his audience of country people of their Irish identity. They were possessors of a history of poetry and song in their own language, much older than that of their conquerors. The dispossessed and depressed could hold their heads a little higher for the rich and witty verse of their own poet.

Great statesmen in the Irish and British parliaments, such as Edmund Burke and Henry Grattan, both Protestant, eloquently led the fight for justice and reform. Protestant leaders of the United Irishmen, such as Henry Joy McCracken, Robert Emmet, Lord Edward Fitzgerald and Wolfe Tone, gave their lives in the fight for freedom and justice around the turn of the 19th century. McCracken and Emmet were executed; Fitzgerald was fatally wounded and captured in March 1798, and died in his cell; Tone, after being sentenced to hanging, drawing, and quartering, committed suicide in his Dublin cell in 1798.

There were many Protestant landlords and churchmen who were active in efforts to alleviate the plight of the Irish poor. George Berkeley, Bishop of Cloyne, was among the liberal-minded leaders preaching toleration of Catholics. As early as 1725, Edward Synge, the son of an archbishop not famous for his sympathy for Catholics, urged repeal of the use of coercive measures against Catholics, in a sermon before the Irish House of Commons. But the liberals, in the last analysis, were too few. Long-established vested interests whetted by bribery even led the landlord class to abandon the Irish Parliament. With the Act of Union of 1801, "independent Ireland" was traded for rule from London in a United Kingdom.

THE EXODUS

It is unlikely that the Act of Union had meant much, for better or worse, for the Fitzgeralds and Harrigans of the remote Mizen Peninsula. They were far from the intrigues of Dublin politics as they prepared for their journey to the New World in 1830-31, and they were among the very few Catholics with the means to get away.

Their departure was described indirectly by the respondents to the *Poor Inquiry.* The Reverend Robert Traill reported that ninety families emigrated in 1831, of a parish population of 13,668. Forty left in 1832, and about twelve in 1833. "They were, with few exceptions," he said, "Protestants, and in comfortable circumstances." Father James Barry reported similarly: "The emigrants were tradesmen, hardy labourers, and farmers with from 20 to 60 pounds capital [but] few of the last class." Richard Notter of Kilmoe testified that "the emigres are of a better description; in fact, most of the people here, who could afford to emigrate, would do so." As to where the fortunate emigrants had gone, the answer was "almost universally to the British settlements in North America."

At many small ports were timber ships from Canada, ready to take passengers on the return voyage. The sharp drop in passenger fares in the late 1820s made emigration possible for the Harrigans and Fitzgeralds, who perhaps had leases to sell and money accumulated from carpentry.

It was time to go. In 1830, Patrick Fitzgerald was 21, brother William was 20, and several other brothers were nearing adulthood. Further division of the land meant impoverishment. The Sullivans, sharing a leasehold with Tim Harrigan in Derryleary, faced the same problem and may have been the first to leave. By the time of the Great Famine no Harrigans, Fitzgeralds, or Kingstons, and few Sullivans and Donovans, were occupiers in Drinane and Derryleary, but those names are found in abundance in North Esk Parish, Northumberland County, New Brunswick, "the Miramichi."

Ellen Sauntry, married daughter of Dennis Harrigan, remained behind with her family, and so did Ellen Lucey, sister of Dennis. In 1848, William Sauntry died near Ballydehob, probably of famine fever. His widow Ellen and seven children (including future Minnesota lumber baron William Jr.) would join their relatives in New Brunswick a few years later, and so would the family of Ellen Lucey.

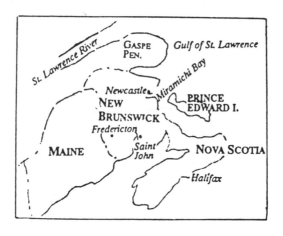

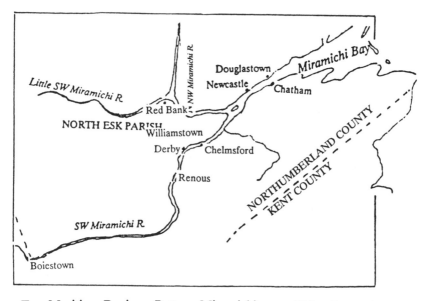

Top: Maritime Region. *Bottom*: Miramichi area of New Brunswick, including Williamstown Settlement in North Esk Parish.

Chapter 2

The Exodus to Miramichi, New Brunswick 1830-51

Until recent years very little has been written about the Canadian experience of Irish immigrants who avoided the cities and settled on the farms and river systems. A study of the tiny Williamstown Settlement in Northumberland County, New Brunswick, gives us some insight into what life was like for these lumberers and farmers, many of whom lived for a generation and more in New Brunswick and contributed enormously to its economy, as they did later to the economy of the American and Canadian West. The study of Williamstown also reveals how Old World prejudices transported to the New contributed to the destruction of a teacher, a school, and a community, after an unfounded charge of child molestation was raised.

The sharp reduction in passenger fares on timber ships returning to British North America about 1830, from five pounds per person to as low as one pound, made possible the first mass emigration of the Irish and mainly Catholic poor.

Ports of embarcation for West Corkonians in 1830 could be Bantry, Crookhaven, Baltimore, and even the tidal harbor of Ballydehob where an emigrant vessel was freighted occasionally.

But Mary Ann Fitzgerald Blake, when she was 102 years of age in Oshkosh, Wisconsin, recalled her voyage at age seven to New Brunswick. She remembered the "crying among the women" during the six weeks on a sailing ship. Few passenger lists for this period have been located, but the entries for Mary Ann and her close relatives might be reconstructed from data on the 1851 New Brunswick census, giving date of entry into the colony:

SPRING/SUMMER
1830

William Fitzgerald	44
Ann (Harrigan)	41
James	15
Maurice	13
Mary Ann	7
Michael	5
Daniel	1

1830-31

John Harrigan	30
Cornelius Harrigan	(adult)

MAY 1831

Patrick Fitzgerald	22
John Fitzgerald	12

JULY 1831

Dennis Harrigan	51
Catherine (Driscoll)	49
Ann	20
John William	18
Catherine	15
Michael	11
Cornelius	8
William	6
Jeremiah	4
Mary	2
Patrick	1
Wm. Fitzgerald, Jr.	20

The great bay which drains the Southwest and Northwest Miramichi rivers must have been a welcome sight for the little girl. But much hardship was ahead for her family. They were in a strange land. They spoke Irish as a first language. They were unused to the ax, needed for construction of log cabins, and had to adjust to a climate which, by the standards of the Mizen Peninsula where an occasional palm tree flourished, was extremely hostile.

MIRAMICHI

The origin of the word "Miramichi" (pronounced MURRUH-muh-SHEE) is debatable. Some think, without convincing evidence, that it is derived from a Montagnais Indian word applied to their hereditary foes, the Micmacs, meaning "County of the Bad People." But to the Micmacs Miramichi may have meant the "Land of Happy Retreat" because of its good hunting and fishing. The word became synonymous with Northumberland County which, at the time of the arrival of Fitzgeralds and Harrigans from West Cork in 1830, contained only ten thousand people on 3,200,000 acres. Perhaps as little as fifteen thousand acres had been cleared (only 27,000 acres by 1840 when the population had grown to 14,600).

The Irish, both Catholic and Protestant, began arriving in Miramichi before 1800. Immigration stepped up considerably after 1815. Grants of free land ended totally in 1829 on the eve of the greatest flood of Catholics, one year before the arrival of our subjects.

The Fitzgeralds and Harrigans found that the best lots on the river systems were already occupied, and they may have worked for several years on the docks of Newcastle or Douglastown, which were thriving. Those towns had been destroyed by the Great Miramichi Fire of 1825, but had been rapidly rebuilt. By 1830, shipbuilding was a major industry in the two towns, and in Chatham across the bay. The yards of William Abrams, James Fraser, Francis Peabody (later taken over by James Russell and in 1838 by the famed Joseph Cunard) were very busy. The sailing ships of these firms were world renowned.

How the small band of relatives from West Cork fared from 1830 to 1835 is unknown. The records are silent except for a few entries on the baptismal register of St. Patrick's Church in Nelson. A daughter, Catherine, was born to William Fitzgerald in 1832, and baptized seventeen months later, on October 6, 1833. Baptized on the same day was Catherine's cousin, Dennis Harrigan Jr., age thirteen months, the last child of Dennis and Catherine (Driscoll). One day Dennis Jr. would have a grandson known to the world as Bing Crosby. The officiating priest was Father William Dollard, soon to become the first bishop of the new Diocese of New Brunswick. Ann Fitzgerald, the last child of William and Ann, was baptized at six months of age on August 9, 1835.

The first appearance of the Harrigans and Fitzgeralds on property records is in 1835, for the remote inland settlement of
Williamstown.

WILLIAMSTOWN

The story of the Williamstown Settlement is typical of many
communities settled by the Irish in New Brunswick and the other
Maritime provinces, whose sons and daughters eventually went
westward in great numbers.

Williamstown has never been heralded as a tourist attraction,
even during the Irish Festivals of recent years sponsored by The Irish
Canadian Cultural Association of New Brunswick. But one historian
of the Miramichi, W. D. Hamilton, now an emeritus professor, University of New Brunswick at Fredericton, has written that it is "the
most interesting of the settlements in the Nor'West," because of its
colorful, although short, history and because so many of the descendants of its old settlers achieved distinction in a number of fields.

REMOTE SETTLEMENT

The settlement is situated inland between the South West and
North West Miramichi Rivers, about six miles west of where these
great rivers converge at Wilson's Point and flow into Miramichi Bay.
Even at its height, if that word is appropriate, in the 1840s, not more
than twenty families lived there, on lots of one hundred and two
hundred acres. There were scattered log cabins. Much land had
been cleared for tillage and several farms, despite marginal soil and
climate, were considered to be flourishing.

GHOST TOWN

Today the land is mostly scrub. A few occupied houses remain,
one being the residence of Gladys Mahoney, widow of Frank
Mahoney, a descendant of early settlers. Many dwellings, abandoned long ago, have become playthings of the wind and rain. It is a
ghost community, and the ghosts are many. One such ghost is that

Williamstown Road (1990)

Abandoned home (1979) of Con Regan, son of John Regan and Margaret Lucey.

Con's grave, Red Bank (1992): "Cornelius Regan - 1846-1924 - Lord have mercy on his soul." [actually 1843-1924] The priest forbid Con's mourners to carry his casket through the cemetery gate. It was lifted over the fence for burial in an isolated corner.

of old bachelor Cornelius Regan, whose deteriorating hut was still standing in 1982. Old-timers can recall Con's death at age eighty-one in 1924. They say that Father Frederick C. Ryan, pastor of the church at Red Bank, would not allow the coffin of old Con to be carried through the main entrance to the cemetery. Con's mourners had to hoist the box over the fence of St. Thomas Cemetery, where it was buried in a remote corner.

Another unhappy ghost is that of James Evers, Williamstown's first Catholic schoolmaster, who held classes in the 1840s in a dwelling belonging to one of the Fitzgeralds on what is now Mahoney property. Evers was accused by a Protestant parent of defiling one or more of the girls in his class, of which more later. The crumbled remains of the fireplace of a Fitzgerald log cabin, possibly the one used for the school, now lie hidden in the brush.

"The land was never any good," said old-time resident Brian Mahoney, brother of Frank, in 1979 shortly before his death. That was one of the reasons for the decline of the community. Another was the ups and downs of the lumber industry on which the community depended, the residents being loggers in the winter and farmers in the spring and summer. A third reason was bitter religious factional fighting between Protestants and Catholics.

THE IRISH METHODISTS

The surnames of the first Methodist settlers in Williamstown are familiar ones on the Miramichi today: Tweedie, McLean, Quayle, Hosford, Graham. The Tweedies were weavers and farmers from County Leitrim. The McLeans and Quayles also had Leitrim roots. The Hosfords may have come from Bandon in County Cork. Why they left Ireland is open to conjecture but one can make educated guesses. These families, way back, had been awarded large tracts of land in Ireland for serving in or financially supporting English armies who waged war against rebellious Irish subjects, especially in the 1640s and 1690s.

As generations passed, there was less and less land to be inherited by individual descendants of the original Protestant adventurers, and some of them could hardly be distinguished in their poverty from their Catholic neighbors. With the end of the Napoleonic Wars in 1815 and the opening up again of European trade ports, there was a steep decline in grain prices in Ireland, which had fed the English military during the wars, and a long general depression was the result. Compounding the problem were the periodic failures of the potato crop. Particularly severe ones occurred in the early 1820s and 1830s. Moreover, the important cottage industry of linen-weaving, the men doing the weaving and the women the spinning, declined radically during the 1820s. These farmers and weavers began emigrating in considerable numbers. They took the six-week passage on the sailing ships plying the timber trade route between British North America and Ireland.

For whatever reasons, some hardy Protestants from Leitrim began arriving on the Miramichi in 1822. They were not the first by any means. Scots and Irish had been settling since the 1760s and by 1822 occupied most of the desirable lots on the rivers.

The first of the Williamstown party was Robert Tweedie, a weaver, accompanied by his large family from Lisduff townland near Carrick-on-Shannon. They arrived in 1822. By 1831, Robert and his brothers Joseph and James and their relative John McLean and his son Joseph had been granted lots of approximately 200 acres each in Williamstown. Another relative, William Quayle, came in 1825, having sailed with his wife and six children on the lumber vessel *Maria of Harrington*. Quayle had served in His Majesty's 10th Regiment of Militia, enduring, according to family folklore, "all the hardships of the Irish Rebellion of 1798." William Graham arrived in June 1824, soon marrying Jane McLean, daughter of John. William and Benjamin Hosford landed in 1831, married Margaret and Mary Tweedie, obtained land grants in Williamstown, and took their places in the Methodist community. Nathaniel Buck arrived from Foxcroft, Maine, marrying Elizabeth Quayle in 1831.

HISTORY OF FRICTION

To understand the friction that later developed between the

Methodists and the Catholics of Williamstown, one needs to know something about the background in Ireland of the senior Methodist settler, Robert Tweedie (1785-1855), and his brothers. They were the great-great grandchildren of an army officer from Tweeddale, Scotland, who fought with the forces of Protestant King William III, which defeated those of deposed Catholic King James II at the Battle of the Boyne in 1690. For his services, Robert was rewarded with land in Ireland. In County Leitrim he and his descendants, although masters for a time of large land holdings, were immersed in a sea of Catholic neighbors and small leaseholders. Their tightly knit Protestant enclave became religiously attuned to the preachings of the Wesley brothers in the mid-18th century.

Many families like the Tweedies understandably developed a siege mentality and a contempt not only for the religion of the dispossessed but also for the "Irish race." There is some evidence that the Tweedies brought this contempt with them to the New World and transplanted it. Robert Tweedie's daughter Isabelle (1830-1915) wrote to a nephew in 1901 expressing her own and her late father's low opinion of Irish Catholics:

When I was a thoughtless girl at home [in Williamstown] our work brought us in contact with rather poor specimens of the Emerald Isle, so I took no interest in the race....I have heard my father tell a minister we used to have, a converted Catholic, there was not a drop of Celtish blood in his veins and say he was Anglo-Saxon, pure Scotch on both sides.

Mixed with this contempt, however, was a feeling of nostalgia for the land which had been the family's home for five generations. One of the immigrant members of the Tweedie family recalled the weeping as the family said farewell to friends at the River Shannon. The Tweedies sustained themselves, she said, during fearful storms on their voyage across the Atlantic by singing a favorite Methodist hymn:

> *Away with our sorrow and fear,*
> *We soon shall recover our home.*

The home they found in New Brunswick could hardly be considered desirable. Since the river-front lots upstream were already occupied by earlier settlers, they were obliged to settle inland in a totally unoccupied area of the old Davidson and Cort grant of the 1760s, divided into lots for settlement but accessible only by a narrow trail. Outsiders labelled the place "Irish Settlement," to distinguish it from "English Settlement," a small community of Methodists from Devonshire, on the North West Miramichi River. However, the settlement soon came to be known as Williamstown, perhaps for William IV, who assumed the throne in 1830, but possibly for William III of the Battle of the Boyne to whom the Tweedie brothers' forebear was indebted for his land in Ireland.

It was tough going for these first settlers. The land had to be cleared, the trees felled and cut and burnt. For many years the planting was done on land covered by tree stumps. Every year a few more acres would be cleared.

METHODIST PREACHER ARRIVES

The Methodists were as fervent in their religion as they were in clearing their land. A circuit-riding Methodist preacher, Reverend John B. Strong of Fredericton, took notes of a visit to the isolated settlement in August 1828. He was greeted by Robert Tweedie and his wife and eight children. They had not seen a Methodist preacher in five years. Mrs. Tweedie wept for joy. "Have I once more fixed my eyes on a Methodist preacher?" she cried. Her children went scurrying to bring the neighbors the good news. Mr. Strong preached a sermon in Tweedie's log cabin and recorded the experience in his notebook:

This good man [Robert Tweedie] was the leader of a little band who had not left their religion behind them in Ireland. For five years he had by means of class-meetings and other simple services, kept the home fires burning as they all prayed for ministers of their own loved church to come and work among them....In this log dwelling, these Irish Methodists told the story of their trials in their adopted country. During the settlers' five years in the woods, their faith in God and attachment to the Church of their childhood had been well tested. Persistence in a religious life had encouraged each other to await the arrival of a minister of their own denomination.

Commenting critically on the nearby Baptist Church, which already had its own minister and church structure on the North West Miramichi, the Reverend Strong praised the Irish Methodists for their stout resistance to the heresy of baptism by immersion:

Immersionist theories had in vain been urged upon them with a zeal worthy of a more important cause, while they thus looked for a messenger of the churches.

The truth was that some of the Methodists did affiliate themselves with the Baptists for a short time, full immersion or no. The affiliation may have been an uncomfortable one for Ann Nutley, who married Tweedie's nephew Joseph McLean in a Baptist ceremony in December 1826. Less than two weeks after the ceremony, the following entry appears in the Baptist Church record book:

Ann Nutley, now McLean, for imprudent conduct is under censure of the church, and Brethren James Tozer and John Woodworth are appointed to converse with her and make report.

The nature of Ann's offense is unknown. The censures recorded in the church book are frequent, and for what Christians today would probably consider very minor imperfections.

DISTINGUISHED DESCENDANTS

In any case, Wesleyan Methodism flourished in Williamstown. For some years a log building was used as both a school and church. Three of the thirteen children of Robert Tweedie and Sarah Dowler became Methodist ministers. Among their great-grandchildren was Thomas Mitchell Tweedie (1872-1944), Chief Justice of the Supreme Court of Alberta. A grandson was Lemuel Tweedie (1849-1917), who served as Lieutenant Governor of New Brunswick from 1907 to 1912. Another grandson was William Morley Tweedie, who taught English Literature at Mount Allison University for fifty years. A grandson of original settler James Tweedie (1794-1863) was Hedley

Tweedie (1866-1950), assistant in opthalmology at Johns Hopkins University for many years, who later had a private practice in Rockland, Maine.   Hedley never forgot his roots in the Williamstown community. For many years he returned to deliver an annual address at the little church.

Perley Quayle, described by Professor W.D. Hamilton as a "teacher and scholar," kept the original Quayle grant under cultivation until his death in 1975, 150 years after the arrival of his pioneer ancestor. His widow was residing in Williamstown in 1983, among a handful of the descendants of the earliest settlers.

The hard-working and God-fearing pioneer Methodists of County Leitrim sank deep roots in Miramichi. These roots were deeper than those of the Irish Catholics from the parishes of Schull and Goleen on the Mizen Peninsula of southernmost Ireland who began arriving in Williamstown in the early 1830s and began departing for the West a generation later. The culture of these Corkonians, in language, religion, attitude toward England, and even in the manner of sharing the land, was not compatible with the cultural soil the evangelizing Methodists wished to fertilize. That is the subject of the next part of the Williamstown story.

THE IRISH CATHOLICS

By 1835, William Fitzgerald and two adult sons were paying taxes on three 100-acre lots in the Williamstown Settlement, about fifteen miles west of Newcastle. They were joined by more Fitzgeralds and Harrigans and by other close relatives and friends from Cork's Mizen Peninsula, some arriving as late as 1852: Regans, Jardines, Kingstons, Sullivans, O'Briens, and Sauntrys. It was a large extended family, a *cineadh* or *derbfine*, which transplanted itself to the New Brunswick colony over the course of about twenty years.

The family seems to have had little trouble acquiring lots in Lower Williamstown, mostly east of Stewart Brook, the Catholic part of the small settlement. John Harrigan (either a brother or son of Dennis) and William Fitzgerald Jr. were listed on an 1838 record as "freeholders by grant of the Crown," but the lots seem to have been shared freely as common property with other members of the *derbfine* in line with the rundale system of rural Ireland. (See Appendix C: Rundale in West Cork.) On an August 1835 tax list, the name of Patrick Fitzgerald, oldest son of William, was listed consecutively with two more "Fitzgerald" entries (no first names given), and one "Harrigan" (no first name), and Michael O'Brien. The four lots were each assessed one shilling six pence.

In 1838, the Catholic and Protestant settlers joined hands in the face of a common threat to their community. Rowland Crocker of nearby Crocker Settlement had diverted the waters of what he called Crocker Lake and what the Williamstown residents called Williamstown Lake, thus severely depleting the water in a brook that flowed through Williamstown. On December 21, 1838, seventeen Williamstown residents addressed a petition to the Lieutenant Governor in Fredericton. They testified that they were all farmers during the summer season and "in the winter cut and haul a few logs off of their farms into the ....mill stream and drive the logs down into Mr. [Jared] Tozer's mill pond which is and has been a great benefit to the Settlement." The petitioners "have learned that Mr. Rowland Crocker has cut a new out let for the water of [Williamstown] lake and has carried and diverted the [water] to the South West instead of allowing it to flow in its natural and accustomed channel whereby the quantity of water is very much less in the....brook and stream and should the [water] be allowed to remain in its diverted state it will not only be injurious to the inhabitants of Williamstown....but ruinous to the said Jared Tozer."

The petition was signed by five McLeans (Arthur, Robert, Joseph, Michael, John), three Fitzgeralds (William, Patrick, John), four Harrigans (William, Cornelius, John, Dennis), and by John Regan, Joseph Tweedy, Jonathan Gillis, George McCombs, and Michael O'Brien. What attention Fredericton gave to the petition is unknown.

Dennis Harrigan served as Overseer of Highways from 1839 to 1846, according to the minutes of the Court of Quarter Sessions at Newcastle, evidence that Catholics were entering the "mainstream."

In 1839, Patrick Fitzgerald attempted unsuccessfully to obtain additional land in the adjoining all-Protestant Crocker Settlement. He was preparing for his marriage to childhood sweetheart Catherine Driscoll, who had arrived from Ireland in that year. On March 25, 1839, Patrick filed a land petition in Chatham, addressed to the Lieutenant Governor. "The land," he petitioned, "is in its natural wilderness state, no improvements having been made thereon." He offered to pay two shillings six pence per acre for the 100-acre parcel "adjoining....Roland Crocker's lot." He was surprised to be informed, shortly thereafter, that his bid was rejected. An application had allegedly been filed earlier by William Craig.

Patrick and Catherine married in November. They remained in Williamstown until about 1850, when they joined Patrick's cousin, John Harrigan, and his widowed mother in Chelmsford on the south side of the South West Miramichi (in 1847, John's father, Cornelius Harrigan, had purchased a lot there from George Flett). John shared the farm with Patrick and his family for a number of years, before Patrick joined his parents, sisters, and brothers in Oshkosh, Wisconsin.

The practice of the Catholic families, generally disregarding legal titles and sharing lots freely with other members of the extended family as some arrived from Ireland and others moved on to Maine and Wisconsin, was in sharp contrast with the practice of the Williamstown Protestants who quickly obtained legal title to individual lots in the English manner.

Language also set the two groups apart. The Catholic settlers, although bilingual, used Gaelic as their first language. To the Methodists of Williamstown the sight and sound of Irish-speaking Catholics coming down the narrow trail in the 1830s to take up land in their community could not have been a pleasant one.

The major divider, however, was religion. Catholics were as firmly set in their faith as the Methodists. They were regularly served by priests of St. Patrick's at Nelson and later by priests of St. Thomas at Red Bank. The marriage and baptismal registers tell the story of the importance of the Church to these early immigrants.

Above all, perhaps, they were interested in education for their children. In Williamstown until 1845 they were hampered by the fact, much as in Ireland, that the official school was, in every sense of the word, a Protestant school, taught by Methodists zealous in their desire to win souls for Christ. For them, the Catholics, worshipping as they did in the Popish institution, were among the souls that needed winning.

CATHOLIC VERSUS METHODIST

The first school in Williamstown, opened in 1838, also served as a Methodist chapel. The teachers from 1838 to 1840 were devout Methodists Sidney Fayle and his wife Margaret Howe. The school returns for the two 1839 terms show twenty-two and twenty-three pupils, all Methodists. The teacher for 1841-42 was Catherine Tweedie, believed to be the daughter of Methodist clergyman J. R. McGeary of County Down. Before 1845 only two Catholic children appear on the returns, and then only for a single term. Some Catholic children, especially Harrigans and Fitzgeralds, can be found during those years on returns for Miramichi schools located at inconvenient distances from their homes. It is most likely that the Catholic parents were distrustful of Methodist instruction.

To understand their fear and their dilemma, one needs to know something about the evangelical zeal of the Methodists of those days. Inspired by the teachings of the Wesley brothers, the Methodists were tireless proselytizers, spreading the Good News of Salvation to all ears they could find. The Reverend D. F. Hoddinott in *From Whence We Came*, a book about Methodist and Presbyterian traditions on the Miramichi, writes that the early Methodist preachers, imbued with the buoyant spirit of the Wesleyan Movement, "felt themselves called of God to win men and women to a personal experience in Jesus Christ and their work was judged not by attendance at services or financial income, but by the number of persons who were led to take a 'stand for Christ.'"

The Methodists must have found their Catholic neighbors to be a stubborn lot, if they attempted any evangelizing. It is likely that they shared the feelings of their leader Robert Tweedie who boasted of his "pure Anglo-Saxon, pure Scotch" heritage. Small wonder that the Williamstown Catholics were not eager to send their offspring to a school administered by Tweedie's band. Their attitude seems to have changed with the arrival of schoolmaster James Howe, brother of Margaret Fayle. Howe was a native of County Tipperary with many years of teaching experience in Miramichi schools. Although a Methodist, Howe had enough of the trust of the Catholics for them to raise the largest portion of the twenty pounds to pay him and to entrust their children to him, no doubt with the understanding that there would be no proselytizing. It was quite customary in New Brunswick at the time, to the dismay of officials in Fredericton, for the parents to negotiate privately for a schoolmaster and then report his being hired as a *fait accompli* to the local trustees.

That Howe may not have had the complete trust of the Catholic parents is suggested, however, by the attendance for the six-month term ending January 13, 1845, of Maurice Fitzgerald, age twenty-nine (age shown erroneously as twenty on Howe's return), himself literate, in a class of children ages five to fifteen, quite possibly monitoring Howe's instruction. Twenty-one of Howe's thirty-two pupils were Catholic, as evidenced from his January 2, 1846, return. Curiously, the children of only two Protestant families, the McLeans and the Bucks, appear on Howe's last return. Some Protestants seem to have preferred schools in nearby settlements with mostly Protestant pupils. Some may have decided to continue the education of their children in a private home.

THE CATHOLIC SCHOOLMASTER

Howe's school was conveniently located just across the road from Protestant Joseph McLean's log cabin. McLean's children were in attendance during Howe's tenure, and were enrolled in the class of Howe's successor, Catholic James Evers, whose first six-month term in Williamstown began on April 30, 1846. McLean became upset, however, by Evers' removal of the instruction to a cabin vacated by "the young Fitzgerald" (which could mean Patrick,

Maurice, or William, elder sons of William Senior). Shortly after this move, McLean withdrew his five children from the school and raised the dreadful charge that Evers was guilty of conduct of the "grossest nature" and of "defiling" one or more of the girls at the school.

The charge was not unique in New Brunswick, and teachers then, as today, were especially vulnerable to it. In 1832, William Beckwith, a schoolmaster in the Parish of Waterborough in Queen's County, was found guilty, after an investigation by three school trustees and the Court of General Sessions (five justices of the peace), of "inconsistent conduct in the school, by indecently touching and interfering with female children under his tuition, and endeavouring to corrupt and deprave their morals, virtue and modesty." The investigators recommended in a report to Lieutenant Governor and Commander-in-Chief of the Province Sir Archibald Campbell, Baronet, that Beckwith be deprived of his license. In 1848, William Ferguson, schoolmaster in the Parish of Delaford [?], was dismissed by the trustees, pending a hearing on charges of "indecent behavior to his scholars."

In the case of Evers the charge was astonishing in view of his age and long service in the community. An Irish immigrant and bachelor in his sixties, Evers had obtained his teaching license for New Brunswick in 1830. He had taught for fourteen years, most of them at nearby Red Bank, before coming to Williamstown. He had successfully applied for renewal of his license in 1842. His application was accompanied by glowing testimonials to his competence and character by the three members of the Northumberland County Board of Education, all Protestants, including Presbyterian minister James Souter, and by the Catholic priest of Nelson, Father Michael Egan. They testified that Evers "had taught at a parish school in North Esk since the year 1830....he is correct and praiseworthy in conduct, strictly attentive to his duties as a teacher....of peaceable and sober habits." The records show that Evers accepted more pupils tuition-free than did any of the other schoolmasters in North Esk Parish. The Catholic church registers at Nelson and Red Bank indicate that he was chosen by many Catholic parents to be godfather to their children. He never received any negative comments, as did at least two other parish teachers, in a column provided for that purpose on forms submitted over the years by the trustees authorizing his government pay bounty (these records are abundant, although not complete). The considerable evidence suggests that Evers was one of the better, more reliable, and competent teachers at a time when many lesser pedagogues were at work in Miramichi schools.

This favorable view of Evers was confirmed by the three North Esk Parish trustees – Anthony Rogers, Robert Forsyth, and John Dunnett – all Protestant but non-Methodist, under whose jurisdiction Evers served both at Red Bank and Williamstown. It was further confirmed by the investigation they conducted immediately after McLean raised his charges in early 1847. They took testimony from pupils and parents under oath, concluding unanimously that McLean's charges were totally without foundation in fact. In June 1847 the trustees once again confirmed their confidence in Evers by reporting to the General Sessions that Evers had taught "to our satisfaction" for the spring term, and they again submitted a favorable report after the end of the following term, Evers' last, all after McLean had raised his charge. Evers' roster for his final term listed the children of the Protestant Buck family. Joseph McLean had been the only parent to withdraw his children from the school.

VENDETTA AGAINST THE TEACHER

But Joseph McLean was not to be denied. Although repudiated by local school trustees and parents for his baseless charges, he decided to take his case independently to a Fredericton bureaucracy with its share of anti-Catholic bias, including a willingness to believe the worst about Papists and Popery and with an equal willingness to play the "Orange card" against the Green. In November 1847, McLean travelled the ninety miles to Fredericton to raise his personal protest before Provincial Secretary John Simcoe Saunders, signing an affidavit which included among other fabrications the half-truth that "the Protestant children with the exception of one family have been withdrawn" from Evers' school.

It is perhaps not surprising that Saunders proceeded to act against the Catholic teacher on the word of one Protestant farmer alone. Saunders was a member of an old Loyalist family from Virginia notorious for its hostile attitude toward Catholics. The secretary's father, Judge John Saunders, is remembered by historians for his poorly drafted judicial opinions and for the severity of his sentencing of Irish laborers involved in the Riot of 1822. So hostile was the judge to Catholics that, on February 27, 1830, he had entered in the record of the Legislative Assembly a statement opposing the Catholic Emancipation Act for New Brunswick, which paralleled legislation passed by the British Parliament (for Ireland) the previous year. The judge's statement, something of a tirade, included the following observation:

It is therefore not only unnecessary but highly impolitic to pass such a law here, which cannot fail to nourish into vigour the influence of that [Roman Catholic] dogma, and thereby introduce a separate organized body, actuated by the same spirit of hostility to our Protestant religion and government, which occasioned the commission of so many atrocities in Ireland.

That Provincial Secretary John Simcoe Saunders, to whom McLean appealed, had inherited his father's prejudices, there can be little doubt. Just four months before McLean appeared with his complaint against Williamstown's first Catholic schoolmaster, Saunders had written his own son, then traveling in Europe, that "the whole country is swarming with Irish Emigrants – not the kind that are likely to be of any uses – either as servants or settlers but will chiefly have to be maintained at the public expense" (July 12, 1847, letter in Harriet Irving Library, University of New Brunswick at Fredericton, in which Saunders also discusses a bloody fracas that day between the Orange and Green).

McLean had found a receptive ear. On the same day, November 16, 1847, that McLean registered his personal grievance, unsupported by any documentation or by corroborating witnesses, Saunders placed a tiny announcement in *The Royal Gazette* that James Evers' teaching license had been "revoked," no reasons given.

The Williamstown school was closed for the following spring, 1848. The trustees, on orders from Saunders, were obliged to re-open the investigation. Obviously very annoyed with McLean and with Secretary Saunders, they sent a scathing letter to Fredericton, pointing out several bold lies in McLean's affidavit, and declaring:

[we have] carefully perused the deposition of Joseph McLean....but consider it unnecessary to go into an investigation....again as we investigated the matter before on the same charges preferred by the same individuals under oath in April 1847 ....all was hearsay and his [McLean's] two sons being required to name the parties with whom Evers was in the habit of behaving indecently towards, and those that were crying on account of his conduct; and they having done so; we gave Evers an opportunity of rebutting the charges, which he did by bringing forward some of the children that attended the school; these we examined on oath....and all denied having seen or heard any such transactions as spoken of by McLean's boys in the most positive manner....[Evers] also brought forward the fathers and mothers of the children who all stated that they had, after hearing the report, taken much trouble to ascertain the truth and all were convinced [of] its incorrectness....we did not remove the School from the Schoolhouse as stated by McLean, neither was it done by our orders, neither do we know when it was Removed, but at the time of the examination spoken of Evers was teaching in an unoccupied private house [belonging to "young Fitzgerald," according to McLean's affidavit] in the middle of the district as appointed by the trustees....as to Evers defiling a girl at the school, if McLean knows who it was he had better name her as we know nothing of the matter and cannot investigate it.

The report was signed by all three trustees on February 7, 1848. Three days later, however, trustee John Dunnett had second thoughts. Behind the backs of the other trustees who had charged him with forwarding the report to Fredericton, but who he now claimed were unavailable for consultation, he appended a minority report. In it, he excused himself for not being able to get the support of the other trustees and raised a totally unsubstantiated new accusation against Evers. The schoolmaster, he said, had been charged four years previously with similar misconduct at Red Bank [almost certainly untrue, according to this writer's research]. "There is no doubt," wrote Dunnett, "that Evers has got many of the Irish Roman Catholics on his side, but I am confident in my opinion that he is not fit to have children under his care."

A few days before, on February 4, James Evers had submitted the following petition to the House of Assembly at Fredericton, in a firm and attractive hand:

The Petition of James Evers of the Parish of North Esk County of Northumberland humbly Sheweth, That your Petitioner is a Schoolmaster and has Taught a School in the Parish of North Esk for the last seventeen years, that in the year one thousand eight hundred and forty two your Petitioner got his Licence renewed, which Licence bears date the twenty seventh day of December one thousand eight hundred and forty-two, That your Petitioner has taught under said Licence ever since and always had his certificate signed by the Trustees until the recent January Session, That your Petitioner applied to the Trustees of the said Sessions to sign his certificate for the last Six Months he had Taught which time ended on the twenty second day of December last and they the Trustees informed him they could not as your Petitioner's Licence had been Discontinued by the Government. This your petitioner found to be true but is up to the present moment entirely ignorant of the cause except by report, your Petitioner having heard causally [sic] that the Government had ordered the Trustees to investigate this matter, called on one of them recently namely John Dennet [the Dunnet name is pronounced *den-net* on the Miramichi] who informed your Petitioner that one Joseph McLean of said Parish had made an Affidavit against him accusing him of improper conduct in his School, your Petitioner requested a Copy of the Affidavit which said Dennet refused, he then requested Mr. Dennet to read the affidavit, this also was denied. Your Petitioner is forced to conclude that his case is singular in the Extreme in many particulars, first in suspending his Licence on the ex parte statements of an individual who to say the least of him does not stand high for Veracity where he is known, secondly in taking away his Licence first and then sometime after ordering an investigation, and thirdly in not sending him a Copy of the charges prepared against or ordering the Trustees to furnish him with one, your Petitioner would court an investigation of any charges that might be brought against him by Joseph McLean or any one else, but as he had no power to move in the matter he is reluctantly compelled to wait their time which may never come, as the Trustees have on a former occasion investigated charges prepared against your Petitioner by the said Joseph McLean and found them entirely without foundation, and your Petitioner is lead to believe that the said McLean has renewed the same charges against him.

Your Petitioner therefore would most Humbly pray that your Honours would take his case into your favourable consideration and grant him the sum of ten pounds as a compensation for teaching a School for the last six Months.

And as in duty bound will ever pray. /s/ James Evers

Evers' plight reminds us of the central character in Franz Kafka's haunting novel *The Trial*, about a man who seeks in vain to learn the nature of the crime for which he has been called to court and for which he is about to be punished. There is nothing Kafka-esque, however, about the response of thirteen Williamstown residents who were quick to sign a petition to accompany Evers' own petition to Fredericton:

We the undersigned inhabitants of this Parish of North Esk residing in the lower Williamstown Settlement, do certify that James Evers has Taught a School in our Settlement for the last twelve Months ending the twenty second day of December last entirely to our satisfaction, and We consider him a Man of good moral character, and We would wish to have him continue as our Schoolmaster providing he could obtain his Licence again. /s/ Nathaniel Buck, Dennis Horagan, Patrick Fitzgerald, John Jordan [spelled *Jardine* on other records], John [his mark] Regan, William Nathaniel Buck, William Fitzgerald, Richard Jordan, Michael Harrigan, Bridget [her mark] O Bryan, William John Horrogan, Michal Sullivan, Patrick Harragan.

The variant spellings of the same surname were typical of the

Return

of the Number of Scholars Taught by James Evers in
District N° 10. in the Parish of Northesk in the County
of Northumberland for Six Months ending the
22ᵈ day of December in the year of our Lord 1847.

N°	Names of Boys	Age	N°	Names of Girls	Age
	Patrick Herrigan	16		Elizabeth Herrigan	16
	Dennis Herrigan	14		Bridget Kenny	14
	David Sheasgreen	21		Sarah Buck	12
	William Buck	14		Harriet Buck	10
	John Fitzgerald	11		Ruth Buck	8
	William Fitzgerald	6		Elizabeth Buck	6
	James Fitzgerald	4		Mary Regan	6
	Cornelius O'Brien	9		Mary O'Brien	9
	John O'Brien	11		Margaret O'Brien	7
	John Fitzgerald, Less	4			
	Cornelius Regan	11			
	Daniel Fitzgerald	7			
	William Fitzgerald, Less	6			
	Alexander Taylor	10			
	Francis Taylor	8			
16	John Kingston	9	9		

Boys — 16
Girls — 9
The Whole   25   James Evers
                           Teacher

To Thomas H. Peters Esqr.
        Chatham

Return of schoolmaster James Evers, for 6 months ending Dec. 22, 1847, Parish of
North Esk, Northumberland Co.   Provincial Archives of New Brunswick,
Fredericton.

We the undersigned inhabitants of the Parish of North-Esk residing in the lower Williamstown settlement, do certify that James Evers has Taught a School in our settlement for the last twelve Months ending the twenty second day of December last entirely to our satisfaction, and We consider him a Man of good moral character, and We would wish to have him continue as our Schoolmaster providing he could obtain his Licence again. Dated this fourth day of February one thousand eight hundred and forty eight.

Nathaniel Buck

Dennis Horrigan
Patrick Fitzgerald
John Jordan
John X Kegan
        his
        mark

Witness Nathaniel Buck
William Fitzgerald
Richard Jordan
Michael Harrigan
Bridget X O'Bryen
        her
        mark
Witness John Horrigan
        his
        mark
Michel Sullivan
Patrick Harrogan

Petition of Williamstown residents, February 4, 1848. House of Assembly Sessional Records, Fredericton, New Brunswick.

times. The signature of Nathaniel Buck, a Protestant, headed the list, and the petition is in his handwriting. The signers included almost all the parents of Evers' pupils, as well as two senior pupils, Patrick Harrigan and William Nathaniel Buck.

On February 22, the petitions from Evers and his supporters were introduced to the House of Assembly by Martin Cranney of Chatham, Miramichi's first Catholic Assemblyman. But it was not until May that the Provincial Board of Trustees in Fredericton, into whose hands the Assembly had placed the matter, acted. On that day they appointed three Northumberland County justices of the peace (Henry B. Allison, a Newcastle merchant; John T. Williston, millowner of Chatham and a friend of Assemblyman Cranney; and Thomas C. Allan) to get in touch with Evers, furnish him with copies of all documents, and invite him to solicit an investigation of his revoked license, "if he was anxious to proceed with it."

The minutes of the Board do not indicate that Evers at this late date solicited the investigation. By the month of May, the poor teacher must have been in dire straits. Most likely he had "left the country," as later reported, to renew his career. In July 1849, the Court of General Sessions at Newcastle approved the payment of ten pounds to Evers on the recommendation of North Esk trustees James Forsyth, Robert Hutcheson, and George Scott (the latter two having replaced John Dunnett and Anthony Rogers). They testified in a form letter that Evers had been a teacher of "moral and sober habits," that he was "duly licensed," and that he "taught to our satisfaction" during the six-month term ending December 22, 1847.

That is the last factual record of James Evers that has been located. Whether he ever received his final pay is unknown. Where the aging schoolmaster spent his last years and where he found a final resting place are also unknown.

McLean made one more thrust at his Catholic neighbors. On February 16, 1850, he submitted a petition for compensation for an alleged act of arson against his property. The petition was supported by the signatures of eighteen Protestants of Williamstown and Crocker settlements and addressed to the Executive Council in

Fredericton.   McLean claimed that he had been threatened by
Catholics because of his accusations against the schoolmaster. Consequently, his barn and new hay crop were set afire by arsonists. He
was "a poor man with a large family" when in 1847 he swore out a
complaint against the "flagrant and diabolical" conduct of James
Evers. He was only "acting as a parent" with the "welfare of the settlement at heart." The petitioner, in a blatant falsehood, testified
that the inquiry by the three trustees conducted three years past
"supported [McLean's] charges and required that Evers' license be
cancelled."

One can only guess why McLean was able to get eighteen of his
Protestant neighbors to lend their signatures to such a falsehood.
Possibly they were concerned mainly that their poor neighbor get
some recompense for his loss. It is also possible that they did not
read the petition carefully and were not very familiar with the events
three years in the past. (None of them had children in Evers' class.)
In any case, McLean got away with the lie, doubtless because a
Fredericton bureaucracy had short memory of events and was un-
willing to take the time to check the facts. The petitioners asked that
McLean be awarded thirty pounds. The government granted him
ten pounds and ordered an investigation of the alleged arson.

THE DECLINE OF THE COMMUNITY

No record of any investigation has been located. At the time it
was called for, however, the Harrigans and Fitzgeralds began moving
on to Maine and Wisconsin.

Several Catholic families remained in Williamstown, chiefly the
Kingstons, O'Briens, Sullivans, Jardines, and Regans, although some
members of these families also went west. They were joined in
Williamstown by Sauntry relatives from County Cork in the early
1850s.

These Catholics and their Protestant neighbors soon were able
to put the Evers Affair behind them, and some sort of truce occurred. James Howe was brought back to teach. His school roster
for July 1, 1851, shows twenty students - eleven Catholics and nine

Protestants. Three of the Protestants were McLeans and six of the Catholics were Fitzgeralds.

The Methodist-Catholic rivalry flared up once again in the 1890s, when Dennis and Michael Sauntry were successive postmasters and named their post office "Ellenstown," after their mother. A political tug-of-war ensued and in 1897 the post office was moved to James Tweedie's place. But the shrivelled and dying community found it could no longer support a post office. The office was closed permanently in 1912. A grandson of Michael Sauntry, Eugene Sauntry, did his part to keep the community alive. Eugene fathered twenty-three children by two successive wives in Williamstown before his death in 1980 at age eighty-two.

The death of Williamstown would have occurred regardless of James Evers and Joseph McLean and the religious antagonisms. Greater forces were at work. There was the lure of money to be made in the West. There was a severe decline in the New Brunswick lumber industry in the late 1840s after Great Britain had reduced tariffs on timber imported to Britain from the Baltic countries. There was the growing indebtedness typically incurred by lumberman-farmers who were off to distant pine forests and rivers in the winter, neglecting the clearing of land for tillage, and falling more and more in debt to the town merchants. Life in Williamstown and in Miramichi in general was, for the great majority, whether Irish or Scottish or English, Catholic or Protestant, very hard at best.

For those who remained, Miramichi proved in time to be a rather good place. Religious suspicions have long since been buried in favor of a live-and-let-live attitude. Religion, to be sure, is still quite important to Miramichiers, as evidenced by the many churches, sometimes two or three in tiny villages along the river systems. But at recent Irish Festivals, Protestant clergymen and Catholic priests have prayed side by side at ceremonies honoring the Irish pioneers and those who died on the "fever ships." In Newcastle, a civilized gentlemen's agreement to have alternate Catholic and Protestant mayors, observed at least until the late 1960s, worked for many years to everybody's satisfaction.

Visitors to the annual Miramichi Irish Festival in July might enjoy a leisurely drive through Williamstown to the old Methodist Church. The cemetery by the church is neatly kept and one will note the names of the earliest pioneers on the headstones. Drive on a few miles to Red Bank and to the Catholic cemetery at St. Thomas the Apostle Church, also neatly kept. There rest the bones of many of Williamstown's earliest Catholic settlers, although some of the graves, including those of Bing Crosby's great-grandparents, Dennis Harrigan and Catherine Driscoll, have no markers. The visitor might note the grave of old Con Regan whose coffin was denied entrance through the cemetery gate. Eighty-year-old bachelor Con is alone in death as he had been alone in life, but a small stone marks his final resting place in a corner of the cemetery.

Shortly before her death in 1988, Vera Fitzgerald Cowan, age 99 and a great-granddaughter of William Fitzgerald and Ann Harrigan, told this writer that she would say a prayer in Irish for Con, and also for James Evers and Joseph McLean. Vera's father, raised in an Irish-speaking household in Williamstown, the son of Patrick Fitzgerald and Catherine Driscoll of the Mizen Peninsula, was a six-year-old pupil in Evers' fateful class, and no doubt a playmate of Con, also in that class. The Irish tradition remained strong in Vera. She recalled her early childhood in Ashland, Wisconsin, when she sat on the lap of her father, a lumbercamp cook, as he sang to her and recited prayers in the ancient Irish tongue. She remembered hopping off his lap to the command: "Bring me my dooth-een!" (Irish, *dúidín*, small clay pipe). Vera Fitzgerald was truly a child of the Northern Migration Route, from Ireland to the Pacific Northwest. Over the course of several generations, members of her line of the family settled in New Brunswick, Maine, Wisconsin, Minnesota, Washington, and Alaska.

Top: Farrell McCarthy, Newcastle, teacher and founding president in 1982 of the Irish Canadian Cultural Association of New Brunswick, with wife Edna Daley. Both Farrell and Edna have Co. Cork roots. 1988 photo.
Bottom, L to R: Dr. Margaret E. Fitzgerald of New York City and Joseph A. King presenting the first copy of their book *The Uncounted Irish in Canada and the United States* to Premier Frank McKenna of New Brunswick at the official opening of the 1990 annual Irish Festival at Chatham.

Chapter 3

FURTHER WEST

lure of the pine

WISCONSIN, MINNESOTA, WASHINGTON

Maurice Fitzgerald, about thirty-five years of age and unmarried, arrived in Oshkosh, Wisconsin, in 1851. Over the next twenty years he was joined by his parents, all but two of his siblings, and a number of Harrigan, Lucey, and McPartlin cousins, some of whom had settled for a time near Houlton and Presque Isle in Maine. As lumbermen as well as farmers, they were following the rivers and the pines.

Maurice's long-lived sister Mary, who had married Limerick-born James Blake in New Brunswick in 1844, gave a brief account of her journey to Wisconsin to a student writing a paper for a history class at Oshkosh Normal School. In 1855, Mary and James and their five children boarded a boat at Newcastle bound for New York City.

On the trip from New Brunswick, Matilda Blake, infant daughter, died on the boat. The boat stopped and the child was buried on the shores of Nova Scotia on an island. After arriving at Chicago, they came on to Sheboygan, Wisconsin, reaching port after battling a raging storm on Lake Michigan. At Sheboygan they were met by Mrs. Blake's brother, Maurice, and he conducted them across land on horseback to the southern end of Lake Winnebago. There they boarded a boat owned by John Fitzgerald (no relation), the only one on the lake and river in 1855, and came to Oshkosh.

Thousands of Irish followed this route, from New Brunswick to New York City via a Maine port, by rail or river boat to Albany, then by rail or canal boat from there to Buffalo, and then by boat and rail to Chicago and Milwaukee.

DISTINGUISHED DESCENDANTS

Four children of William and Ann Fitzgerald – James, Maurice, Michael, and Daniel, all born on the Mizen Peninsula – made notable successes of themselves as lumbermen and farmers in Oshkosh. Maurice, Dan, and James built large brick homes at Fitzgerald Station, south of Oshkosh. Maurice's house burned down in the 1880s (perhaps poetic justice, if indeed he had been involved in the alleged arson on the Miramichi). But the houses built by Dan and James, county landmarks, still stand. Dan's is the "elegant brick structure" described by Harney in *History of Winnebago County, Wisconsin* (1880).

Of twenty-two granddaughters of William and Ann who lived to maturity, ten became schoolteachers. One of them was Josephine FitzGerald (1858-1931) who spelled her name in the ancient Norman fashion, a leading educator in the Pacific Northwest in charge of teacher training at Cheney College, now Eastern Washington State University.

A grandson, Cecil Bernard Fitzgerald (1882-1972), served as mayor of Seattle in 1919-20 and founded the Washington Motor Coach Company, later sold to Greyhound. Grandson Albert Fitzgerald (1868-1938) served as mayor of Tomahawk, Wisconsin. His younger brother, Cornelius, known as "The Cherry King" of Ferndale, Washington, took the grand prize for cherries at the Alaska-Yukon Exhibition in Seattle.

Grandson Stephen McPartlin (1874-1949) was founder and president of the Union Insulating Company in Chicago and an original director of the Celotex Corporation.

MINNESOTA AND BEYOND

Many cousins and other Irish Catholics from Miramichi, including Harrigans, Sauntrys, Suttons, Mackeys, Walshes, settled in Stillwater, Minnesota, where they played leading roles in the logging, driving, rafting, and sawmill operations of the last quarter of the 19th century. They include Dennis Harrigan Jr. (1832-1915), born and raised in Miramichi, a major building contractor in Minnesota and, later, Washington, and his famous grandsons, Bing and Bob Crosby; Lyman Sutton (1867-1958), great-grandson of Dennis Harrigan Sr., president of the Cosmopolitan State Bank in historic Stillwater, named to the Hall of Fame for his civic service in that town; William and John Harrigan, grandsons of Dennis Sr., and sons of Patrick Harrigan, who founded the Scotch Lumber Company in Fulton, Alabama.

WILLIAM SAUNTRY

One great achiever was William Sauntry Jr., grandson of Dennis Harrigan Sr., and son of his eldest daughter, Ellen. William was baptized by the priest of Schull on September 6, 1845, on the eve of the Great Famine of 1845-48. His life, begun in a great public tragedy, ended in a personal one. A millionaire and leading figure in the logging industry on the St. Croix River in Minnesota, he took his own life with a revolver shot on March 10, 1914, in a St. Paul hotel room. The garish house he built in Stillwater, in the Moorish manner and known as "The Alhambra," has become a major tourist attraction.

BIG JACK LUCEY

An interesting but uncelebrated member of the extended family of this study was Jack Lucey, the robust, six-foot, two hundred pound grandson of Ellen Harrigan Lucey, shot to death by a drinking companion on July 26, 1888, on the streets of St. Paul. The St. Paul newspaper described him the next day as the former proprietor of a "notorious resort in Hurley, Wisconsin [who] has lately been engaged in operating a floating house of ill fame on the Mississippi River between the city and South St. Paul."

A CONCLUSION

The headstones in the old Oshkosh cemetery contain the only record of the deaths of William Fitzgerald and Ann Harrigan (the records and courthouses of Oshkosh, known as Sawdust City, regularly burned down in the last half of the 19th century):

Stillwater Gazette November 18, 1914

REVOLVER SHOT ENDS HIS LIFE

William Sauntry, For Many Years Executive Head of Vast Lumber Interests, Takes His Life.

Sitting in Easy Chair at Ryan Hotel, St. Paul, Revolver Shot Does Its work

William Sauntry, who at one time and for many years, was the leading spirit in the lumber industry on the waters of the St. Croix, and who managed, as a stockholder and director, the great Weyerhauser interests on the river, ended his life Tuesday night in a room at the Ryan Hotel, St. Paul, a revolver shot accomplishing the act.

No reason for the act of self-destruction has been given, nor is any reason known. Mr. Sauntry was in Stillwater on Monday in consultation with several gentlemen, and his demeanor at that time gave no reason to suppose that he contemplated self-destruction.

Mr. Sauntry left his apartments at the Angus in St. Paul yesterday afternoon, apparently in good health and spirits. He was seen by several acquaintances during the afternoon, none of whom noticed anything out of the ordinary with him.

Mr. Sauntry came into the Ryan last night about six o'clock, registered and was assigned to a room on the third floor. When discovered by an attache of the hotel shortly afterwards, he was sitting in an easy chair, the door to the room being open. The employe of the hotel saw blood on the body and gave the alarm. Mr. Sauntry was breathing when the clerk of the hotel arrived on the scene, but expired shortly after. The bullet from the revolver passed through the roof of the mouth and into the brain, causing almost instantaneous death.

William Sauntry came to Stillwater from Williamstown, Canada, nearly fifty years ago. He found work in the pine woods, where he drove oxen on the drives in the spring and in the harvest fields in the summer. Later, as a result of his thrift and hard work, he accumulated sufficient funds to embark in business for himself, became associated with Albert Tozer, the firm name having been Sauntry & Tozer, and when Mr. Tozer retired Mr. Sauntry purchased his interest in the business. Still later Mr. Sauntry became identified with the great Weyerhauser interests that purchased the immense tracts of standing timber from the late Isaac Staples, and managed the business for his associates at this end of the line. The St. Croix Boom Company stock was leased from the heirs of the late Martin Mower. Mr. Sauntry built the Nevers dam, several miles above Taylors Falls, and the boom was run under his management for many years. Finally Mr. Sauntry disposed of his interests in the Weyerhauser companies, retiring, it is said, with not less than two million dollars. All this, save a few hundred thousands, made in iron mines in the north part of the state, was made in the lumber business. Since that time Mr. Sauntry had sought other fields for his endeavors, and, it is said, was not so fortunate in his investments. For the past several years Mr. Sauntry had made his home in St. Paul.

Surviving are his wife, one son, Beltram Sauntry, a Minneapolis lumber broker, and a sister, Mrs. John Kain, of this city. He was about 67 years of age.

WILLIAM SAUNTRY MANSION AND GYMNASIUM *(626 North Fourth)*

This home is typical of the elaborate homes built by early lumber barons. The Moorish recreation hall behind his non-such mansion has elegantly finished mahogany, beautifully carved in Spanish patterns hanging from the ceilings. There was a vast dance floor, bowling alley and swimming pool. It was said that Mr. Sauntry sent architects to copy the Alhambra. Several sets of double glass doors with stained glass art are spaced around the exterior. *From St. Croix Valley Chamber of Commerce leaflet* •

WILLIAM SAUNTRY, son of William Sauntry Sr. and Ellen Harrigan of Dromkeal Townland near Ballydehob, was baptized at Schull on Sept. 8, 1845, beginning life on the eve of a great public tragedy and ending it in a personal one.

Ann, wife of William Fitzgerald,/died Feb. 25, 1880/aged 99 yrs. 11 mos.; William Fitzgerald/died Aug. 25, 1873/aged 86 years; Joseph M./son of P.&K. McPartlin/died August 15, 1873/age 1 yr. 3 mos.

This book has been an attempt to reconstruct the lives of one extended family in a broad context. It may be useful, as a case study, to historians and to others curious about the Old Country from which their ancestors fled when life became too harsh and unbearable, and about the New World where they pioneered. The lives of these quite ordinary but certainly heroic people deserve to be recorded and remembered with gratitude

"The student of migration," wrote George Stephenson, "will not concern himself with the people on whom fortune has smiled graciously....he will study the documents that portray the spirit, hopes and aspirations of the humble folk who tilled the soil, felled the forest, and tended the loom....the less favored majority in every land."

Chapter 4 and Appendix A are essentially genealogical. It is hoped that they might be helpful to those seeking the elusive parish and townland of their own ancestors.

TOP: Kate O'Sullivan O'Callaghan of Goleen, Co. Cork, with granddaughter Deirdre McKiernan, c1950. Kate emigrated as a teenager to Boston, worked as a domestic, married Daniel O'Callaghan of Fermoy. BOTTOM: Dr. Eoin McKiernan, Kate's son-in-law, with daughter Ethna, 1993. Dr. McKiernan founded the Irish American Cultural Institute of St. Paul, Minnesota; the publication *Eire-Ireland*; and Irish Books and Media of Minneapolis (now headed by Ethna McKiernan). He produced over 100 programs for PBS-TV and in 1982 was elected Honorary Life Member of the Royal Dublin Society, the only American so honored.

Chapter 4

The Search:

Harrigan's Rocks Revisited

This is a personal chapter about the author's search for his roots in Ireland.

CHARLES MARTIN FITZGERALD

My grandfather Charles Martin Fitzgerald was born in Oshkosh, Wisconsin, in 1866, and raised on a farm south of the city. While employed on the ore docks at Ashland, he met and marrried Elizabeth Tyrrell in 1894. Her parents, like her husband's, were Irish-born. Charles was a smart and witty man, a major in the Army during World War I, after which he worked as a civilian in the Army Supply Corps. Elizabeth was an equally wise and witty farm girl from Minnesota. The fortunes or misfortunes of government service brought them to Brooklyn, New York, where their daughter married Joseph Anthony King, also of Irish forebears. They had five children, of whom I was the third.

My grandparents lived to great age. Charles died at 88, Elizabeth at 92. I knew them well and loved them much. I sometimes questioned them about their forebears. Charles said that his father was Maurice Fitzgerald, who died in the early 1880s near Oshkosh. He knew the names of several of his aunts and uncles who also settled in or near Oshkosh, and thought they had all been born in County Cork and had all spent some time in New Brunswick before moving on to Wisconsin long before he was born. He kept in touch with some of his cousins. But he had no folklore, no records, no

Bible, no keepsakes of the New Brunswick or Ireland periods of his ancestors. He did have some old photos, including one of four children, perhaps relatives, taken in Stillwater, Minnesota, but he did not know how they fitted into the family. That photo, however, will play a part in this story, in its place.

ACUTE GENEALOGIA

With this information I began my quest. It was a genealogical project of consuming interest for several years. It involved much travel to archives in the United States, Canada, and Ireland, and the writing of hundreds of letters to distant cousins, librarians, record keepers, local historians, and others. It was also very expensive. In the process I learned, among many other things perhaps interesting only to me, that I was a third-cousin (once-removed) of Bing Crosby.

WISCONSIN RECORDS

The first step on the path to the genealogical Holy Grail (the exact spot in Ireland from whence sprung my ancestors) was to obtain the Winnebago County, Wisconsin, death certificate of Charles' father, Maurice. It indicated his death date in 1884, and the names of his parents, William Fitzgerald and Ann Harrigan. That was my first knowledge of Harrigan being a family name. County Cork was given as Maurice's place of birth, no specifics as to parish.

I then located the Oshkosh grave of Maurice's parents, William and Ann, the headstone indicating they had died in 1873 and 1880.

I proceeded to search all sorts of other records: obituaries, more cemetery records, probate papers, United States censuses from 1850 to 1900 and more, all devoid of information on the New Brunswick and Ireland years. I located the obituaries of several uncles and aunts of my grandfather Charles, and did learn from the obits that the Fitzgeralds had emigrated from Ireland to New Brunswick in 1830. Uncle Mike and his sister Mary (Blake) died in Oshkosh in 1927 and 1926, both over 100 years of age. Obituaries and articles about them in the Oshkosh newspaper indicated that the family had spent a number of years in New Brunswick before they and other members of the family moved on to Maine and to Wisconsin, where they began arriving in the early 1850s.

One interesting bit of information was that Ann Harrigan Fitzgerald, my great-great grandmother, had a sister named "Mrs. Ellen Lucey" who died in Oshkosh "some years ago" at the age of 112, "the oldest woman in the state." I obtained Ellen's death certificate. It indicated that she died in 1891, age 112, birthyear 1779, County Cork, Ireland. Her parents' names, alas, were not recorded. But Ellen Lucey's brief obituary in the local paper noted that she was survived by a son John Lucey, a policeman. John Lucey's own obituary indicated he was born in County Cork in June 1833, the son of Timothy Lucey and Ellen Harrigan. After much sleuthing and letter writing, I located descendants in Wisconsin and Minnesota, but they had less information than I had. I also located many descendants of Great-grandfather Maurice's siblings, score upon score of them. They were equally uninformed about New Brunswick and the Old Ireland years.

NEW BRUNSWICK RECORDS

There was no relief for my curiosity without getting into the New Brunswick records. I started with the entire 1851 census for the Colony of New Brunswick, the first census to give genealogical data of value. It was on microfilm at the Mormon archives in Salt Lake City. The local Mormon library obtained it for me on loan. It consisted of about a dozen reels of film. I turned the crank of the film reader for many hours, many evenings, county by county, eleven of them. Finally, I got to Northumberland County, the last one to be searched. There, in Nelson Parish (northside), were William and Ann Fitzgerald and several of their youngest children. In the same log cabin were their daughter Mary and her husband, James Blake, and their young family. In neighboring North Esk Parish were the families of Patrick, William Jr., and John Fitzgerald, all siblings of Great-grandfather Maurice, listed consecutively with the families of Dennis and Catherine Harrigan and families with surnames O'Brien, Regan, Sullivan, Kingston. These census records indicated that the

Fitzgeralds and Harrigans had come over during the spring and summer months of 1830 and 1831.

Passenger lists are not available for the Miramichi ports of Newcastle and Chatham for this period, but there are many other fascinating records on which my ancestors and their relatives made their marks. The tax lists indicate that the Luceys lived for a time in the 1840s with the Fitzgeralds in North Nelson, now Derby Parish. I learned that Ann Harrigan Fitzgerald had a brother named Cornelius Harrigan and that he raised a large family. I learned from the register at the Catholic church at South Nelson that Ann Harrigan Fitzgerald's two youngest children were born in the New World in 1832 and 1835; and that her brother Dennis Harrigan's youngest child, Dennis Jr., was also born in New Brunswick.

The school rosters for the 1830s and 1840s were a valuable source of confirming evidence. They indicated that these families placed great value on education.

The marriage and baptismal records for these large families, invariably citing the names of witnesses and godparents, pointed to the closeness of the Harrigans, Fitzgeralds, O'Briens, and Sauntrys. The absence of cross-marriages between members of these families suggested that they were indeed close kin. In the one instance where Michael Sauntry, whose grandfather was Dennis Harrigan, married a Fitzgerald, the register reads that a dispensation was granted. They were second cousins (once-removed), outside the prohibitions of canon law, but the priest obtained a dispensation from the bishop nevertheless, perhaps to be on the safe side.

COUSINHOOD OF A SORT

In genealogical research, one always wants to go backward, but sometimes the victim of Acute Genealogia must go forward for a while to relieve the distress, before he can return to his backward path. That is what my data on Dennis Harrigan forced me to do. I traced his son Dennis Jr. to Stillwater, Minnesota, a bustling sawmill town on the St. Croix River, heavy with immigrants from Miramichi, New Brunswick. Dennis and his spouse Catherine Ahearn had seven children between 1867 and 1879, according to the baptismal register of St. Michael's Catholic Church and census records. The third, born in 1873, was named Catherine. Her name meant nothing to me until the newspapers reported the death of Bing Crosby on a golf course in Madrid, Spain, in 1977. One news story mentioned that his mother was born Catherine Harrigan in Minnesota. That was enough for me to take a renewed interest, at my sister Margaret's suggestion, in the 1880-vintage Stillwater photo from our grandfather's collection. Four children had posed for it, two boys and two girls. The oldest, standing, appeared to be about ten. That would have been the age of Catherine Harrigan in the year 1883. The apparent ages of the other three children also corresponded with my records of this family.

I still had to move forward in time, but a stroke of luck soon was to set me again on the backward path so comfortable to genealogists. The luck was a letter from Margaret Harrigan Kendall of Redmond, Washington. She had been given my address by a Stillwater, Minnesota, librarian, with whom we had both corresponded. She mentioned that she was a first cousin of the late Bing and his brother Bob, the bandleader, and that she too was seeking her Harrigan roots. She wondered who I was. She possessed a letter from a deceased uncle indicating that the Harrigans and Fitzgeralds were "first cousins"; that they had been born on "a small farm in County Cork"; that the "first Harrigan" was John of Skibbereen, who also used the surname O'Brien and was known as Organ O'Brien because he played the organ beautifully in the church at Skibbereen; that the Harrigans and Fitzgeralds settled together in Miramichi, New Brunswick, before moving on to such places as Oshkosh, Wisconsin, and Stillwater, Minnesota. She included in her letter the California address of her cousin Bob Crosby and his wife June.

I mailed Margaret and Bob copies of the Stillwater photo and other data. Bob immediately recognized the older girl in the picture as his mother. He was delighted with it, never before having seen such an early photo of her. I presented him with the original.

VISIT WITH BRIAN MAHONEY

It was now time for a visit to Miramichi, New Brunswick. There in 1978, in the community of Williamstown, now little more than a ghost town ten miles west of Newcastle, I met Brian Mahoney. He was well in his 70s and the descendant of old settlers. He claimed to be related to both Harrigans and Fitzgeralds way back. He had been told so by his long-lived schoolteacher grandmother, Annie Donoghue O'Brien. Without prompting, he remembered from his boyhood a very old man named Mick Sauntry. Mick, he said, had in his old age made a visit back to the village of his birth, "Bally-dee-hall, ten miles west of Skibbereen." By this time, I knew from the records that Michael (Mick) Sauntry was a son of William Sauntry and Ellen Harrigan, and thus blood relatives of my Harrigans. Brian told me that a grandson of Michael had raised a family of twenty-three children, surely a local record, by two consecutive wives. His second wife and some of the children still lived just down the road. I have since met several of these twenty-three children, twenty-two of whom were still alive in the mid-1980s.

BALLYDEHOB AND SCHULL, WEST CORK

I wasted no time consulting a map of West Cork. There, ten miles west of Skibbereen, was the village of Ballydehob, and a few miles south was the village of Schull. Neither did I delay writing to the priests of the two parishes that served this area on Ireland's southernmost peninsula, at Schull and Goleen. The Schull registers of marriages and baptisms are extant from 1807, but with large gaps during the next two decades. The extant Goleen registers start in 1827. The parish priests kindly searched the barely legible and deteriorating records and came up with a treasury of information.

The records revealed the baptisms of three children of Dennis "Horgan" and Catherine Driscoll between 1811 and 1813, and two more in 1829 and 1830; the marriage of their oldest daughter, Ellen, to William Sauntry in 1828; and the baptisms of six of their children between the years 1829 and 1845. One of the six was Michael Sauntry, baptized in 1830, the man from "Ballydehall" remembered by old

Brian Mahoney of New Brunswick. The names of the children from these families corresponded exactly, and the birth years almost always exactly, with New World records.

The records also revealed the baptisms of two children of Timothy Lucey and Ellen Horgan in 1810 and 1813 and of another (John, their youngest) in June 1833, corresponding precisely with the information on John Lucey's Oshkosh, Wisconsin, death certificate.

I next consulted the *Tithe Applotment Books*. Prepared in the 1820s, these records were an attempt to list all occupiers of land (except in the cities) in Ireland by townland and parish, for the purpose of taxing them to support the established Protestant Church of Ireland. In 1827, Daniel "Horragan" and James Fitzgerald, no doubt senior members of their families, were listed as joint occupiers of twenty-two acres in Drinane Mor townland, civil parish of Schull (West Division), and were obligated to pay a tithe of 19 shillings and 7 pence. "Horragan" and "Harrigan," along with Sullivan and Kingston, appeared as the surnames of occupiers in nearby Drinane Beg and Derryleary townlands, and Luceys were also thereabouts. The townlands of Derryleary and Drinane were on the border of the Catholic parishes of Schull and Goleen. Just off the coast of Derryleary, according to an Ordnance Survey map, were the outcroppings known as Harrigan's Rocks.

Although the names of my direct ancestors, William Fitzgerald and Ann Harrigan, were not found on these records (see Notes to Chapter 1, "Records"), the names of Ann's sister and brother and of a number of her nieces and nephews on the registers of Goleen and Schull were strong circumstantial evidence of Ann's roots on the Mizen Peninsula.

The next step on this genealogical odyssey was to determine the present-day occupiers of the old Fitzgerald and Harrigan farms. From the Rates Office in Cork City, I learned that the present occupiers of the townland of Drinane were Denis Declan O'Mahony and Michael Donovan; and that nobody had paid taxes on Harrigan's Rocks for one hundred years. I soon learned through correspondence with distant cousin-in-law Mary Margaret Lucey of Ratooragh, Schull,that the Harrigans of long ago had weed-cutting rights to the rocks. The weeds were used for fertilizer.

It was time to write a book, *The Irish Lumberman-Farmer,* published in 1982. It contains extensive family charts, an index of several hundred surnames, and quite a bit of background historical data. Two newspaper editors in Cork City and in Skibbereen thought their readers would be interested in just how Corkonians had been getting along in America; so I was asked to write full-page stories for both papers, all about the roots on the Mizen Peninsula of its most famous American son, Bing Crosby. The editors included my own photo, next to Cousin Bing.

It was also time to visit West Cork for a lecture to the West Cork Archaeological and Historical Society, and for an autographing session arranged by Jack O'Connell of Schull Books, my distributor. The society wanted to hear about the Corkonians of yore and how their descendants were doing. The Society's witty president, Michael Donovan, assuring me that Harrigan's Rocks were mine for the asking, offered to act as my caretaker. Soon thereafter, he wrote me a comforting letter about how the rocks had "weathered a fine storm and taken on a nice shine." As an honorarium, the Society commissioned a local artist to do an oil painting of Harrigan's Rocks. It is today proudly displayed in the King living room.

THE LAND TODAY

My visit had been memorable, meeting Mary Margaret Lucey and her brother Con, Mike Donovan, and Declan O'Mahony. It was good to know that an O'Mahony was once again prospering on land confiscated from the O'Mahonys almost 350 years ago. Declan pointed out the ruins of what once was, according to tradition, a carpenter shop, and a cluster of stone cabins, probably once the dwellings of carpenters William Fitzgerald and Dennis Harrigan.

It was a short distance to Derryleary Townland where Harrigan's Rocks lie just off the coast in Toormore Bay. I was told that the Hulls, who leased the forlorn rocks to the Harrigans, were not fondly remembered in local folklore. The last local occupier bearing the name appears to have been the Richard Edward Hull who, in 1876, was reported in *Returns of Owners of Land* to be the owner of 2,671 acres in County Cork.

The lead-lined coffin of Hull, who reportedly died in the 1880s, was placed in a vault at the entrance to the old graveyard on the Colla Road. A local historian informed me that the grave was desecrated during World War II by someone who removed both the remains of Hull and the saleable lead from the coffin. Hull's house at Leamcon has had several owners in more recent years, despite the belief a Hull haunts the place to this day. An estate agent told the author that "on two separate occasions I showed the place to prospective buyers and they got a most unfavourable reaction from whatever vibes were flying around in it, although they didn't know anything about its reputation for being haunted."

Jack Roycroft pointed out the old cemetery on his land near Lowertown where the Luceys, Harrigans, and Fitzgeralds buried their dead long ago. The inscriptions on the weathered stones, half-hidden in the weeds, are unreadable today. When he was a boy, Jack discovered a *souterrain* (underground chamber and tunnel) containing a skull beneath the cemetery. That chamber may have been the very "cave" where Ellen Harrigan hid with her family in 1798.

Mary Margaret Lucey produced an old snapshot of her aunt and another woman in Massachusetts. The other woman turned out to be the mother-in-law of Dr. Eoin McKiernan, distinguished scholar and founder of the Irish American Cultural Institute of St. Paul, Minnesota, and the journal *Eire-Ireland*. Eoin was delighted to get a copy of the photo.

My wife and I hiked to the top of Mount Gabriel where we viewed Schull Harbor, my ancestral farm a few miles to the southwest, Cape Clear far out beyond Roaring Water Bay, and many miles of the grand coastline of southernmost Ireland.

THE GENESIS OF MYTHOLOGY

On a Sunday we drove to Bantry for a musical evening. The

Historic Mass celebrated in June 1982 at the Mass Rock near Schull, County Cork, on property of Bob O'Regan of Cooradarrigan. Priests officiating (left to right): An t-Ath Daithi Ó Foghlu, Denis Kehily, and Patrick Hickey. *Bottom*: the congregation stands in the rain. *Cork Examiner* photo, June 27, 1982.

Ruins of cottage with storage shelf, Drinane Townland, Schull, property of Declan O'Mahony. 1983 photo by Betty King.

View from Mount Gabriel, Co. Cork, author J.A. King in foreground, Schull Harbor and Cape Clear in background. 1983 photo by Betty King.

master of ceremonies in the pub was married to the head of the local historical society with whom I had corresponded. At one point he stopped the entertainment to introduce the "cousin of Bing Crosby, come here all the way from California." Nameless, I accepted the applause as modestly as I could. "His wife and his sister are here beside him." More polite applause. "I've been introduced many times," my sister said later, "but never as the sister of the cousin of Bing Crosby."

Then there was a conversation my wife and sister had with a friendly lady on the little pier at Schull the next day. Not associating my sister with the "cousin of Bing" but clearly proud of her community, the lady said, "Do you know that Bing Crosby was born here?" She had obviously read one or another article of mine on the subject of Bing's roots published in the *Cork Examiner* and the *Skibbereen Southern Star*, which revealed that Bing's *great-grandfather* was born on the Mizen. So, there is always some truth in folklore. Well, almost.

MASS ROCK

On June 27, 1982, three priests–Fathers Denis Kehily, Daithu Ó Foghlu, and Patrick Hickey–said Mass on the local Mass Rock in the mountains, at Cooradarrigan near Schull. Speaking after the Mass, local historian C.G.F. McCarthy recalled the days when it was necessary to hide the priest and place a sentry.

It is fitting, I think, to conclude this chapter–and this book–with a note of respect for the tough but gentle people of southwest Ireland. If an explanation is needed for the achievement in the New World of so many Corkonians, it will not be found in the suggestion of the distinguished American historian Merle Curti (*The Making of an American Community*) that the exposure of the Gael to the Englishman and his language somehow stimulated the poor creature to greater achievement. A better answer can be found on a mountainside in the remote parish of Schull in rural Ireland on a rainy Sunday in June.

Appendix A

A Genealogical Study
HARRIGANS AND CROSBYS

This genealogical record of Bing Crosby's maternal ancestors should be of some historical interest, tracing as it does, over the course of three generations, the Northern Migration Route from Ireland through New Brunswick, Maine, Wisconsin, and Minnesota to the Pacific Northwest. We have therefore included the research in this appendix.

Bing Crosby had at least a passing interest in his Irish roots. The late Father John Deasy, Parish Priest of Schull, told the author that Bing had made some inquiries but did not have precise enough information for a successful search.

One problem, it turned out, was that Bing thought his grandfather was born in Ireland, whereas he was actually born in New Brunswick. This inaccuracy appears on the January 7, 1964, California death certificate of Bing's mother, Catherine Crosby. Her father's name is given as Dennis Harrigan, birthplace Ireland. Another problem was that Bing's grandfather and great grandfather both bore the name Dennis Harrigan, usually "Horgan" on the Irish records.

BING'S GREAT-GREAT GRANDFATHER
Bing Crosby's earliest known ancestor, the "first Harrigan" according to a family tradition, bore the name John. He was born in the mid-1700s but his name appears on no records that have as yet been discovered. Two of his sons each named their first son John and their first daughter Ellen. One of the daughters named her second son John and her second daughter Ellen. The Irish tradition, especially observed by the oldest children, was to name the first four children after the grandparents, paternal first. It is likely then that Bing's earliest known ancestors were John and Ellen Horgan of

County Cork who were married in the 1770s and whose four known children—Dennis, Ellen, Ann, Cornelius—were born after 1778.

Larry Crosby, Bing's oldest brother, was told that John used two surnames, O'Brien and Harrigan. This was not unusual. To distinguish between cousins bearing the same first and last names, wrote folklorist Kevin Danaher, country folk were often identified by the name of their landlord, townland, trade, or "sept" (clan). A natural child raised by a single mother might also be known by the name of both mother and father, if the father were known.

As mentioned in Chapter 1, the Horgan/Harrigan family were small farmers and carpenters who had weed-cutting rights to Harrigan's Rocks in Toormore Bay. According to a story received and passed along by Larry Crosby, John Harrigan was known as "Organ O'Brien" because he played the organ in the church at Skibbereen, a market town some fifteen miles east of the village of Schull. (Skibbereen did have a chapel, perhaps with an organ, as early as 1816. The foundation for the structure that became the pro-cathedral was laid in 1825 and the new church was dedicated by Bishop Collins in 1830.)

Perhaps the Harrigans were members of the larger O'Brien sept. Irish and New Brunswick records indicate that the Harrigans and their Fitzgerald cousins were neighbors and close friends, most likely kinsmen, of O'Brien families in both Ireland and New Brunswick *(see Notes for Chapter 1)*. It is also possible that "Horgan" and "O'Brien" somehow became "Organ O'Brien" in the oral tradition as it was passed on. "Organ" is also a variant of Horgan, Irish *O hArgain*.

Records exist for several of John's children, including Ellen, Dennis, and Ann, birth years from 1778 to 1782 according to United States and Canadian records. Also Cornelius, birth year unknown; and perhaps a fifth child, John, born about 1800. Ellen married Timothy Lucey; Dennis married Catherine Driscoll; Ann married William Fitzgerald; Cornelius married Elizabeth Sloan in New Brunswick; John married Ellen Murphy in New Brunswick.

GREAT-GRANDPARENTS

Bing's great-grandparents were Dennis Harrigan (abt 1781-abt 1867) and Catherine Driscoll (abt 1782-abt 1864). They are probably buried in an unmarked grave by the church of St. Thomas the Apostle at Red Bank, Miramichi, New Brunswick.   Dennis and Catherine married about 1808 and had ten children before emigrating in 1831. Their eleventh and last child, the only one born in the New World, was Dennis Jr., born in 1832.

The composition of the family, put together from Irish and New World records, follows (the surname is spelled variously on early New Brunswick records, e.g., *Horigan, Hourigan*):

1. Ellen (abt 1808-1897), married William Sauntry in 1828, Goleen Parish, County Cork.
2. Ann (1811-1857), married Patrick Keys.
3. John William (1813-alive 1871).
4. Catherine (1816-1893), married William Walsh.
5. Michael (abt 1820-1882), married Elizabeth Walsh.
6. Cornelius (abt 1823-alive 1903), unmarried.
7. William (abt 1825-abt 1875), married Jane Gallagher.
8. Jeremiah (abt 1827-1903), married Margaret Murray.
9. Mary (1829-   ).
10. Patrick (1830-abt 1924), married Catherine Hogan.
11. Dennis (1832-1915), married Catherine Ahearn.

The baptisms of Ann, John, and Catherine are recorded on the register of the Roman Catholic Parish of Schull:

September 16, 1811: Ann Horgan, daughter of Denis and Catherine (Driscoll). Sponsors: Thomas Lancer, Ellen O'Heas.
November 20, 1813: John Horgan, son of Denis and Catherine (Driscoll). Sponsors: Michael Driscoll, Ann Lancer.
May 6, 1816: Catherine Horgan, daughter of Denis and Catherine (Driscoll). Sponsors: James Lucey, Peg Goggin.

The baptisms of two more of their children are recorded on the register of neighboring Goleen Parish:

March 25, 1829: Mary Horgan, daughter of Denis and Catherine (Driscoll). Sponsors: Jerry Murray, Mary Harrington.
March 13, 1830: Patrick Horgan, son of Den[is] and Catherine (Driscoll). Sponsors: Dan Driscoll, Joan Lucey.

The marriage of the oldest daughter, Ellen, to William Sauntry of Dromkeal townland near the village of Ballydehob, was entered on the register of Goleen Parish by Father L. O'Sullivan (mentioned in the "Religious Feuding Amidst Famine" sub-section of Chapter 2).

February 1828 (exact day gone from deteriorated register, but about 10th of February): William Sauntry and Ellen Horgan. Witnesses: Denis Sauntry and D. Horgan.

On *Griffiths Valuations* (1848-64), William Sauntry was listed as leasing a house and garden on 40 perches of land (a small fraction of one acre) at Dromkeal from Robert Swanton. This poor cottier could not have known before his death in 1848, probably of famine fever, that his youngest child, William Jr., would one day become the lumber baron known as the "King of the Saint Croix" in Minnesota. Baptisms of six of the eight children of William Sauntry and Ellen Horgan are recorded on the Schull register, including that of William Jr., baptized in 1845 (see obit, Chapter 3, p. 76).

BING'S GRANDPARENTS

The baptism of Dennis Jr., the youngest child of Dennis Harrigan and Catherine Driscoll and the only one not born in Ireland, is recorded on the register of St. Patrick's Catholic Church in Nelson-Miramichi, New Brunswick, October 6, 1833, age given as thirteen months, sponsors Patrick Fitzgerald (a first cousin, son of Ann Harrigan Fitzgerald) and Joanne Burchell.

Dennis Harrigan Jr. married Catherine Ahearn (daughter of Irish-born John Ahearn and Ann Meighan, early Miramichi settlers) about 1866, when his occupation was given on New Brunswick directories as "brewer" at North Esk Boom. Shortly after the marriage, Dennis and Catherine moved to Stillwater, Minnesota, a sawmill town on the St. Croix River. There, from 1867 to 1880, Dennis pursued the trade of carpenter and building contractor. From 1881 to 1884 he was living in Knife Falls (now Cloquet) where he was a church trustee and a partner in the construction of the first Catholic Church building. He also erected the first Methodist and

Presbyterian churches in this town. He then contracted for some structures in St. Paul, where the family resided at 765 Hawthorne Street (in a house built by Dennis, still standing in 1982). Dennis and his oldest son William moved to Tacoma, Washington, in 1888, and the rest of the family followed in 1889. There he pursued his career as a building contractor and later as an inspector. He died in Tacoma on September 18, 1915, his obituary noting that he was an active member of the Knights of Columbus. His wife Catherine passed away in 1918. The children of Dennis Harrigan Jr. and Catherine Ahearn were all born in Minnesota. The baptisms of five of them (asterisked below) appear on the register of St. Michael's Catholic Church in Stillwater:

*1. William John Harrigan (1867-1949), married Anna T.

 2. Alexander Ambrose (abt 1869-alive in 1915).
*3. Edward (1870-1926), married Dolly J. Levings.
*4. Catherine (1873-1964), married Harry Lowe Crosby.
 5. Anne (1875-alive 1964), married Ed. J. Walsh.
*6. Francis Albert (1876-alive in 1915), married____.
*7. George Leo (1879-abt 1955), married Hannah E. Anderson.

PARENTS

Catherine Harrigan, Bing's mother, was born above the old creamery just north of the Lowell Inn in Stillwater, Minnesota, on February 7, 1873. She was baptized on February 11 at St. Michael's Church, the sponsors being Michael Kinsella and Catherine Mary Dunn. She died on January 7, 1964, at Santa Monica, California.

Catherine Harrigan married Harry Lowe Crosby, a bookkeeper, in 1894 in Tacoma, Washington. Harry, a Protestant with roots going back to a 17th century sea-faring family in New England, converted to Catholicism. The family moved to Spokane in 1913. The seven children of this marriage are as follows:

1. Laurence Earl, "Larry" Crosby (1895-1975).
2. Everett Nathaniel Crosby (1896-1966), baptized May 2, 1896, St. Leo's, Tacoma.
3. Henry Edward, "Ted" Crosby (1900-1973), baptized August 12, 1900, St. Patrick's, Tacoma.
4. Harry Lillis "Bing" Crosby (1903-1977), baptized May 31,

Folklore: John Harrigan also was known as "Organ O'Brien" because "he played the organ so beautifully in the church at Skibbereen."

* marriage recorded at Goleen
+ baptism recorded at Schull
# baptism recorded at Goleen

John HARRIGAN (HORGAN)
m Ellen?
4 known children

Dennis HARRIGAN
c1780-c1864 d NB
m Cath Driscoll
emig 1831 to NB
10 ch

- *Ellen Harrigan c1808-97 m Wm. SAUNTRY
- +Mary 1810-
- +Ellen 1813-
- +John Wm. 1813-f1871 unmarried
- +Cath. 1816-93 m Wm. WALSH
- Michael 1820-82 m Eliz. Walsh
- Cornelius 1823-f1895
- William 1825-77 m Jane Gallagher
- Jeremiah c1827-1905 m Margt. Murray
- +Mary 1829-
- +Patrick 1830-1924? m Cath. Hogan
- Dennis 1832-1915 m Cath. Ahearn

Ellen Harrigan
c1779/89-1891
m Timothy LUCEY
arrived Maine 1851
10 ch, 6 known

- m James FEELEY
- James c1826-1903 m Mary Ann O'Leary
- Catherine c1829-91 m SULLIVAN
- Timothy c1829-1903 m Anna Maria O'Leary
- #John 1833-1909 arrived Maine 1851 m Margt. Neville
- (?)Michael Lucey, sponsor at bap. of dau of John Lucey, Houlton, Me., 1867

Ann Harrigan
c1780/90-1880
m Wm. FITZGERALD
emig 1830 to NB
10 or 11 ch

- Patrick c1809-93 m Cath. Driscoll
- William 1811-98 m. Isabella Scott
- James 1815-1910 m Mary A. Geoghegan
- Maurice c1815-1884 m Johanna Cassin
- John c1819-c1854 m Julia Goggin
- Mary c1823-1926 m James BLAKE
- Michael c1825-1927 m Ellen Derby
- Daniel c1829-1888 m Eliz. Casey
- Catherine 1832-1923 m Patrick MCPARTLIN
- Ann 1835-1918 m Joseph FARRELL

Cornelius HARRIGAN
d. bet. 1852-1861
bur. St. Patk., Nelson
m Eliz. Sloan in NB
9 ch

- Elizabeth c1831-
- Mary c1832-
- Ellen/Eleanor c1834-
- Ann c1836-
- John c1837-1908 m Cath. Fitzpatrick
- Daniel c1838-1924
- Jane c1842-
- James c1847-1923 m Hannah
- Alexander 1849-d young

c = approx.
f = alive

**John HARRIGAN 1801-f1851 emig 1830 m Ellen Murphy in 1836 NB 6 ch: Timothy, 1837; Jeremiah, 1838; Bridget, 1840; Cath., 1841; Helena, 1843; Honora, 1848

**John Harrigan & Ellen Murphy were sps. with Patk. Fitzgerald & Cath. Driscoll at bap. of two oldest ch. of Wm. Fitzgerald/Isabella Scott in 1840, St. Patrick's Ch. register, Nelson NB

1833

B, 186,

Catharine

Fitzgerald

357

On the sixth of October eighteen hundred *&t Fifth* I have baptised Catharine aged seventeen months of the lawful marriage of William Fitzgerald *&t* Horigan. The Sponsors being Michael Brian & Anne Horigan.

W. Dollard *Pa*

B, 187,

Denis

Horigan. —

On the sixth of October eighteen hundred thirty three I have baptised Denis aged thirteen months born of the lawful marriage of Denis Horigan and Catharine Driscol. The Sponsors being Patrick Fitzgerald & Joanna Burchill. —

W. Dollard *Pa*

Baptismal records for Dennis Harrigan Jr. and his first cousin, Catherine Fitzgerald, Oct. 6, 1833, St. Patrick's Church, Nelson-Miramichi, New Brunswick. Officiating was Fr. William Dollard, soon to become the first bishop of the new Diocese of New Brunswick.

Dennis Harrigan Jr. (1832-1915) and Catherine Ahearn (1836-1918), grandparents of Bing Crosby.

The Crosby family, 1963, Catherine Harrigan Crosby cutting the cake on her 90th birthday at Bing's house.
Standing, left to right:
June & Bob Crosby
Larry & Elaine Crosby
Mary Rose Crosby Pool
Everett Crosby
Ed Mullin, husband of Catherine
Harry L. "Bing" Crosby
Ted Crosby.
Seated left to right:
Catherine Crosby Mullin
Kathryn Crosby, Bing's wife
Catherine Harrigan Crosby
Florence Crosby, Everett's wife

1903, St. Patrick's, Tacoma. Sponsors: Francis Harrigan, Edith Carley.
5. Catherine Cordelia, born October 3, 1904, now deceased; married Ed Mullin.
6. Mary Rose (1906-1990), born May 3, 1906, married Jim Pool.
7. George Robert "Bob" Crosby (1913-1993), baptized September 7, 1913, St. Aloysius, Spokane; married June Kuhn.

BING

Bing Crosby married Wilma Winifred Wyatt (Dixie Lee) on September 29, 1930, at the Blessed Sacrament Church, Sunset Boulevard, Hollywood. The four children of this marriage are:

1. Gary Evans Crosby, born 1933.
2. Dennis Michael Crosby (1934-1991), a suicide.
3. Phillip Lang Crosby, born 1938.
4. Lindsay Crosby (1938-1989), Phillip's twin, another suicide.

Lindsay Crosby died of a self-inflicted gunshot wound in the head eleven days after learning that the inheritance with which he supported his family had run out.

Dixie died of cancer on November 1, 1952, on her forty-first birthday. Five years later, on October 24, 1957, Bing married Olive Grandstaff (Kathryn Grant) at St. Anne's Catholic Church, Las Vegas, Nevada. The three children of this marriage are:

1. Harry Lillis Crosby Jr., born 1958.
2. Mary Frances Crosby, born 1959, m. Edmund Lattimer.
3. Nathaniel Patrick Crosby, born 1961.

Mention should be made of Bing's brother Bob Crosby, a great musician in his own right, but who lived for so long in the shadow of Bing. Bob's wife, June Kuhn, died in March 1992, and Bob in April of the following year. They had five children: Cathy, Chris, Robert Jr., Stephen, and Malia. June and Bob were always helpful to this writer in his genealogical pursuits.

Appendix B: Irish Terminology

Some definitions:

BARONY. Land of a baron, an ancient land division, "often based on the old *Tríocha Céad* or Gaelic lordship," says Diarmuid Ó Murchadha; several in a county and sometimes overlapping county lines, widely used from 16th century onwards for administrative, tax, and regional purposes, its use declining after the 1898 Local Government Act which created a new structure for local government; 273 baronies in Ireland.

CHURCH PARISH. For the established Church of Ireland, frequently the same boundaries as the civil parish; rarely so for the Roman Catholic parishes. The Catholic parish of Goleen included all of the civil parish of Kilmoe and the western section of the civil parish of Schull.

CIVIL PARISH. An administrative jurisdiction containing many townlands; about 2,500 parishes in Ireland. The origin of the civil parish as a geographical division is clouded in uncertainties. "In the East of the country," writes Diarmuid Ó Murchadha, "the (Norman) manor and (civil) parish were normally coincident." It may sometimes correspond with the old Irish *tuath*, the area controlled by a sept or clan. The records indicate that the Normans often used existing Irish land divisions in the redistribution of land. The Mizen Peninsula parishes were Schull and Kilmoe, the latter including the village and Catholic parish of Goleen.

COUNTY. Thirty-two of them in Ireland, each containing many parishes; etymologically, the territory of a count or earl, who sublet to barons; territorial divisions set up for administrative purposes by the English government in Ireland.

DIOCESE. A number of parishes under a bishop; Diocese of Cork for the Catholic parishes on the Mizen; Diocese of Ross (Diocese of Cloyne and Ross after 1835) for the Church of Ireland. Schull and Kilmoe were the Church of Ireland parishes on the Mizen Peninsula; Schull and Goleen were the Catholic parishes.

GNEEVE. 1/12 of a ploughland, enough for eight cows.

IRISH ACRE. About one and a half English or statute acres, more or less. Falley and others say 1.62 to the English acre, but this figure often does not correspond to the reality of the actual conversion to English acres, especially after the Ordnance Survey in the 1840s. Some have defined an Irish acre as the area one man could plough in a day with a pair of yokes; divided into the *rood* (four per acre) and the *perch* (forty per rood). Holdings shown in the Tithe Applotment Books, c1825-35, are given in Irish acres; in Griffith's Valuations, c1850, English acres.

IRISH MILE. Approximately 1.3 English miles.

PLOUGHLAND. Land required for grazing 100 cows, among other definitions, which include "the amount of land a single plough could break up in a year." One ploughland could equal 400 acres and more of land on the Mizen Peninsula.

POUND. Once the basic monetary unit, twenty shillings to the pound, twelve pence to the shilling; a *guinea* was worth one pound plus one shilling.

PROVINCE. Four in Ireland: *Ulster*, nine counties, including the cities of Belfast and Derry (present "Northern Ireland" contains only six of the Ulster counties); *Leinster*, including the city of Dublin; *Munster*, including the city of Cork; *Connacht*, including the city of Galway.

TITHE. The amount that was assessed by law on land occupiers in Ireland to support the established Church of Ireland; after the reform acts of 1823-24, usually set at 10 percent of what a grain crop would yield in value, averaged for seven years, 1815-21.

TOWNLAND. The unit by which head landlords measured their holdings; a shortening of the legal term "town & lands"; sometimes synonymous with ploughland, but usually smaller than the old ploughland. 62,100 townlands in Ireland (1841 census). One of them, Sheskin in Co. Mayo, is 7,102 acres; one in Co. Dublin is less than one acre.

DERIVATION OF SOME PLACE AND PERSONAL NAMES

Bally-, *baile*, place, land, farm

Ballydehob, ford of the two mouths

Beg, *beag*, small

Cork, *corcach*, a marsh

Derryleary, derry from *doire,* oak grove; Leary's oak grove

Drinane, *droighneán*, place of blackthorns

Dublin, *duibh-linn* (duv-lin), black pool; more anciently *Baile-átha-cliath*, pron. "Blaa-clee," place of the hurdles, for the artificial ford constructed at the River Liffey crossing; from *áth*, a ford; *cliath*, a hurdle

Fitzgerald, Norman-French, son of Gerald; prefix *Fitz-* is cognate with modern French *fils,* translated into Irish as Mac, *MacGearailt*

Goleen , little inlet (*-een,* little)

Harrigan, Horgan, *(Ó) hArgáin,* mainly a County Cork name

Kil-, *cill*, church

Knock, *cnoc*, hill

mór, big, great

rath, fort

Ratooragh, from *rattoo*, northern ring fort, plus *ragh*, meaning of which is doubtful

Rossbrin, *Ros Brain*, Bran's headland; a wood or promontory (usually means wood in the South and a peninsula in the North)

Schull, Skull, arguably, school; but perhaps from *scumhal*, precipice or coast indenture

Skibbereen, *An Sciobairín*, meaning unknown

Toormore Bay, *Tuar Mór*, big green field where things are put out to dry or bleach

Appendix C: Rundale in West Cork

According to evidence gathered by the author, the Irish in the parishes of Kilmoe and Schull practiced a modified form of the ancient Gaelic system of "rundale." Under the rundale system, the land was held communally by the *cineadh* (or *derbfine*), the extended family roughly consisting of all those with a common great-grandfather. The family lived in the *clachan*, a cluster of huts which included an "infield" of tillage plots (the size of individual plots depending on family tradition and need) and an "outfield" of common pasturage. The infield was regularly adjusted and re-distributed with deaths, emigration, and spin-offs of new *cinidheacha*.

With the fall of the Gaelic order, the English system of individual ownership was imposed on Ireland. Nevertheless, pockets of rundale remained well into the 19th century despite the English law. Some evidence for this is in the Tithe Applotment Books (TAB), for the civil parishes of Kilmoe (1828) and Schull (1827).

The tithe proctors were supposed to report the lease holdings in acres, setting the exact amount of the tithe for each leaseholder based on a set formula. But most of the occupiers on the Mizen Peninsula measured their land not in acres but in "gneeves." If the pasturage afforded grazing for 100 cows, that was one "ploughland," sometimes synonymous with "townland," which could be as many as 400 acres and more for one ploughland in Schull. If the land could serve eight cows, that was one "gneeve"; one cow, one-eighth of a gneeve.

In 1836, the parish priest of Schull, Father James Barry, reported that the "number of acres [in the parish] cannot be accurately ascertained because the land is let in this country by the 'gneeve', which constitutes, in general, the one-twelfth part of a ploughland....There are very few who hold three 'gneeves' and from that down to one-eighth of a gneeve is the general extent....in many cases the occupier is the third or fourth from the head landlord."

The tithe proctors for Schull and Kilmoe therefore had a real problem in reporting. In Kilmoe, they handled the problem by actually reporting the holdings in gneeves, not acres. In Schull, however, the proctors imposed artificial acreages on groups of households. This became evident to the writer after a close study of the TAB for Schull, where there are many, many such entries as "Joseph Darby and partners" (46 acres); "Timothy Driscoll Sr. and partners" (43 acres). In fact, almost all of the holdings, according to the TAB, are over 20 Irish acres and only 450 leaseholds are listed.

Sometimes the Schull proctors gave the figure in both acres and, parenthetically, in gneeves. Thus for five consecutively listed parcels/leaseholds in Glawn Townland, acreages of 102 to 113 are given, and "3 gneeves" for each. Several household heads are listed for each of the parcels. Sometimes the approximate location of the gneeve-holding is shown, as in Cappaghglass Townland. There, for three consecutive enumerations of 143, 149, and 148 acres (each with several listed household heads), the equivalent in gneeves is also given: "5 gneeves East," "5 gneeves Middle," and "five gneeves West." It is evident that the lines were not clearly drawn.

Further circumstantial evidence that a form of rundale was at work and that the tithe proctors must have had difficulty allowing for it, is suggested by these figures:

1827 TITHE APPLOTMENTS - SCHULL PARISH *(figures gathered by the author from extremely difficult to read film)*
450 parcels/leaseholds enumerated.
1,000 (approx.) occupiers listed by name, sometimes 6 or 7 to a
   parcel; sometimes one or two names followed by "& partners."

1831 CENSUS - SCHULL PARISH
2,308 inhabited houses (65 uninhabited).
2,370 families (therefore, average of 6 persons per house)
14,265 total population (7,117 males, 7,148 females).
Occupations by family: agriculture (and fishing), 2,058; trade, man-
ufacturing, handicrafts, 108; all other groups, 204.

It is evident that less than half of the household heads are listed by name on the 1827 TAB. The census enumerators were able to count houses and, hence, householders without much trouble. The tithe proctors, obliged to think in terms of acres and not houses, were understandably unable to identify exact acreages held by rundale "partners." Consequently, they assigned the tithe to the group or *cineadh*, listing only its most senior members.

The Schull records can therefore be disappointing to genealogists seeking their "ancestral farm." Scores of families can be found on the baptismal and marriage registers that are not listed on the 1827 TAB. For example, five children of Dennis Harrigan and Catherine Driscoll appear on Schull baptismal records between 1811 and 1830, and a daughter on the Goleen marriage register for 1828. Yet Dennis Harrigan is not a listed occupier on the 1827 TAB.

Most likely Dennis was a junior adult member of one of the family groups headed by a Harrigan or "Horragan" in Drinane Mor, Drinane Beg, or Derryleary townland.

This analysis has helped explain a phenomenon the writer has noticed on tithe books he has studied in many remote rural Irish parishes. He has often noticed four or five consecutive listings for occupiers, sometimes all with the same surname, and each of them is occupying the same number of acres, roods and perches. This suggests measurement by convenience rather than reality, and is surely a sign of rundale.

The drastic decimation in population by famine, disease, and emigration after the Great Famine, meant the end of rundale in Schull and elsewhere.

NOTE: *The Ordnance Survey in the 1840s renamed some townlands, eliminated others (which were subsumed by neighboring townlands), and firmed up often fuzzy townland boundaries. One can usually find a "disappeared" townland by comparing surnames and acreages on the TAB with the later c1850 Griffith's Valuations (GV), always allowing for differences between Irish acres (on TAB) and English or statute acres (on GV). Thus two townlands in Schull Parish, Drinane Mor and Drinane Beg with a total of 115 acres, became one townland, simply Drinane, with 156 acres on the GV. Across Roaring Water Bay in Tullagh Parish near Baltimore, Spain Townland of the TAB disappeared altogether, subsumed by Ballymacrown Townland on the GV, as evidenced by surname and acreage analysis.*

Appendix D: "Oldest Woman in Wisconsin"

Ellen Harrigan Lucey (see photo, p. 22)

Everybody knows that some people for their own reasons claim to be younger than they are. Conversely, genealogical research indicates that people of great age for reasons of prestige sometimes claim an even greater age. Ellen Harrigan Lucey was such a person.

Several years before her death in Oshkosh, Wisconsin, on March 25, 1891, at the reported age of 112 (death certificate), Ellen Lucey was locally renowned as "the oldest woman in Wisconsin if not in the United States" (*Oshkosh Weekly Northwestern*, January 19, 1887).

No birth or marriage record has been located for Ellen (Schull Parish baptismal entries begin in 1807, marriages 1809). The Oshkosh paper reported that she was born in Ireland in 1778, married [Timothy Lucey] when she was 22, had ten children, the youngest being John Lucey "born when his mother was fifty four years old." She said she "came to America in 1851 and settled with her husband in the State of Maine" and "four years ago....came west to live with her son, and although then past her 104th year made the journey alone."

The likelihood is that Ellen was about nine or ten years younger than claimed. The baptism of her oldest known child, Mary, was recorded on the Schull Parish register on March 20, 1810; another daughter, Ellen, on October 2, 1813; and her youngest child, John, on the Goleen Parish register, June 2, 1833. If she married at age 22 and had her first child in 1810 and her last in 1833, a birth year of 1788 seems much more likely than 1778.

The arrival in Oshkosh of a woman claiming to be of such great age achieved publicity as far away as New Brunswick. The *Saint John Weekly Freeman* of June 23, 1883, reported: "News was received in St. John last week of the safe arrival of Mrs. Lucy [*sic*], who left Houlton [Maine] May 24th to visit relatives in Oshkosh, Wis. Mrs. Lucy is 104 years of age. She made the long journey unaccompanied by any personal friend."

Oshkosh quickly called attention to the celebrity. The City Directory for 1886-87, which ordinarily listed only name, residence, and occupation, added "Widow of Timothy (107 years of age)" after Ellen's name, at the residence of her son John, a policeman, and his family at 133 Merritt St.

Ellen's great leap in age seems to have come about after she left Maine. On the 1870 census for Littleton, Aroostook County, Maine, her age had been given as 70; on the 1860 census, 60; both consistent with a birth year of 1800, more than ten years *younger* than she actually was.

Ellen was not alone. Other members of her family upped their ages a bit as they approached 100. Ellen's sister, Ann Harrigan Fitzgerald, was reported to be 99 years 11 months in age when she died in Oshkosh on February 19, 1880, meaning a birth in March 1780. But her ten known children were born between 1808 and 1835, suggesting the likelihood that year 1790, not 1780, would be closer to her year of birth. Her age is given as 60 on the 1851 census for North Nelson, New Brunswick, 63 (much too young) on the 1860 census for Oshkosh, and 78 on the 1870 census.

Two of Ann's children, Mary Ann Blake and Michael Fitzgerald, achieved a degree of local fame in Oshkosh in the 1920s by celebrating their 100th birthdays. But they were celebrating, in all truth, a little ahead of time.

Mary died on August 17, 1926, reportedly at 101, her birthday given as January 1, 1825. She was certainly very close to that. Her age was listed as 14 on the March 1840 roster of pupils of school-master James Evers at Red Bank/Cassilis, New Brunswick; age 25 on the 1851 census for Nelson Northside.

Her younger brother Michael, who died on April 4, 1927 at the reported age of 101, claimed he was born on November 1, 1825. But his age is given as only 14 on school returns submitted by William Wilson at Nelson Northside, New Brunswick, in July and August 1841; age 24 on the 1851 census for Nelson Northside; age 22 on the 1850 census for Presque Isle, Aroostook County, Maine; age 27 on the 1860 census, Oshkosh; age 40 (much too young, perhaps because he had recently married a woman in her 20s!) on the 1880 census; age 75 on the 1900 census. It seems likely that Michael upped his age by a year or two, but may have been 100, or just short of it, when he died.

It is no pleasure exposing the harmless fibs of the old ones, wishing to reach age 100 a bit ahead of time. What they did not know is that their contribution to family and society lay not in their longevity but in their lives as pioneers in the New World.

Notes and Bibliography

Notes for Chapter 1: A Parish in West Cork

Records. William Fitzgerald and Ann Harrigan did not emigrate until 1830; yet the records for the Catholic parishes of Schull and Goleen do not show baptisms for any of at least eight children born to them between 1808 and 1829, nor do William and Ann appear as sponsors at any baptisms, including those of the children of Ann's brother Dennis or her sister Ellen (Lucey). It is possible that William and Ann Harrigan, soon after their marriage, settled across Roaring Water Bay between Baltimore and Skibbereen. There, for the civil parish of Tullagh, the *Tithe Applotment Book* for 1828 listed a William and a James Fitzgerald as co-occupiers of a 41-acre farm in Spain Townland (which was later subsumed by Ballymacrown Townland), and they are listed consecutively with O'Briens and Taylors. It is perhaps more than a coincidence that in North Esk Parish, New Brunswick, the William Fitzgerald of this study was also listed consecutively with Taylors and O'Briens (as well as Harrigans) on the tax lists for that parish for 1835 to 1837.

Over-Encumbered Estates. One interesting case is that of the Lord Audley Estate (see W. Neilson Hancock, *On the Causes of the Distress at Skull [Schull] and Skibbereen during the Famine in Ireland.* Dublin, 1850). The huge estate of Lord Audley included the copper mines at Coosheen, Schull, and eastward to Skibbereen. He inherited the estate in 1818 and by 1837 had run up a debt via mortgages, interest, and legal fees, of 167,300 pounds, on an estate whose rentals through a middleman holding a 99-year lease netted Lord Audley only 577 pounds per year. Furthermore, as the year approached when the lease would fall due (1854), the actual value of the properties decreased. Since the law gave all improvements on the properties to the middleman, or to the receivers in bankruptcy, or to a new bidder and owner, there was less and less incentive for the actual occupiers to make improvements on their holdings. Such improvements would have generated sufficient income for the tenant to produce other kinds of food along with the potatoes. Less reliance on potatoes would have meant less distress when that crop failed.

Bibliography for Chapter 1: A Parish in West Cork

Bolster, Evelyn A. *A History of the Diocese of Cork (from the Earliest Times to the Reformation).* 4 vols. Shannon, Ireland, Irish University Press, 1972.
Bowen, Desmond. *The Protestant Crusade in Ireland (1800-1870).*

Dublin, 1978.

Brady, H.M. *Clerical and Parochial Records of Cork, Cloyne, and Ross*, vol. 2 (1896), pp. 247-48; information on Schull and the rectors Anthony and Robert Traill. Also vol. I, p. 176 (1863) for information on Rev. W.A. Fisher and the use of famine relief funds to win converts.

Burke, Rev. William P. *The Irish Priests in the Penal Times (1660-1760)*. Shannon, Ireland, 1968; first published 1914.

Concannon, Mrs. Thomas (Helena). *Irish Nuns in Penal Days*. London, 1931.

Coombes, Rev. James. "Goleen Parish," *The Fold* (Cork diocesan publication). Cork, 1967; and letters to J.A. King, 1980-87.

_____. "The O Mahonys of Ivagha," *The O Mahony Journal*, vol. II, Summer 1981.

_____. *A History of Timoleague and Barryroe*. Timoleague, County Cork, 1981.

Corish, Monsignor Patrick J. *The Catholic Community in the Seventeenth and Eighteenth Centuries*. Dublin, 1981.

_____. "Irish Catholics before the Famine: Patterns and Questions," *Journal of the Wexford Historical Society*, no. 11, 1986-87. Also January 1988 letter to J.A. King.

_____. "The Irish Catholics at the End of the Penal Era," *Religion and Identity*, edited by Terrence Murphy and Cyril J. Byrne. St. John's, Newfoundland, 1987.

Cork County Council, Cork City. Addresses of occupiers, Valuations Books, rated occupiers of land in Schull Parish.

Cork Mercantile Chronicle, items cited by Coombes, Hickey, Bowen; also October 8, 1847 report with Relief Committee figures on deaths and emigrations, September 1846–September 1847.

Deady, John, and Elizabeth Doran, "Prehistoric Copper Mines, Mount Gabriel, County Cork," *Journal of the Cork Historical and Archaeological Society*, no. 225, January/June 1972. But see also O'Brien, William F.

A Dictionary of Irish History 1800-1980, ed. by D.J. Hickey and J.E.Doherty. Dublin, 1980. See "Tithes," 561-62.

Donnelly, James S., Jr. *The Land and the People of Nineteenth-Century Cork*. London and Boston, 1975.

Foster, R.F. *Modern Ireland, 1600-1972*. London, 1988.

Furlong, Nicholas, "The Times and Life of Nicholas Sweetman, Bishop of Ferns," *Journal of the Old Wexford Historical Society*, no. 9, 1983-84.

Hancock, W. Neilson. *On the Causes of the Distress at Skull [Schull] and Skibbereen During the Famine in Ireland*. Dublin, 1850.

Hickey, Rev. Patrick. *A Study of the Four Peninsular Parishes of West Cork, 1796-1855*. Unpublished master's thesis, University

College, Cork, 1980; and letters to J.A. King, 1980-87.

_____. "Fr. Laurence O'Sullivan, P.P., Goleen (1828-48) and *Souper Sullivan* by Eoghan Harris," *The Fold*, April 1986. See also Jim Cluskey, "Controversial TV Series on Famine," *Cork Examiner*, July 15, 1983, and response by Hickey, August 1983 (undated clipping, author's file).

_____. "Famine, Mortality and Emigration: A Profile of Six Parishes in the Poor Law Union of Skibbereen, 1846-47," Chapter 22 in *Cork History and Society*, editors Patrick O'Flanagan and Cornelius G. Buttimer. Geography Publications, Dublin, 1993.

Holland, Rev. W. *History of West Cork and the Diocese of Ross.* Skibbereen, Cork, 1949.

Keena, Catherine A. "Recollections of Mrs. Mary Blake." Manuscript in Oshkosh (Wisconsin) Public Museum, c1926, 3 pp.

Kennedy, Robert E., Jr. *The Irish: Emigration, Marriage and Fertility.* Berkeley and Los Angeles, 1973. Emigration statistics, 1847-1891, p. 27.

King, Joseph A. *The Irish Lumberman-Farmer*, Lafayette, California, 1982.

_____. (with Margaret E. Fitzgerald). *The Uncounted Irish in Canada and the United States.* Toronto, 1990.

_____. "Tracing Bing Crosby's Roots to West Cork," *Southern Star,* Skibbereen, County Cork, June 25, 1983.

_____. "When Irish Eyes Are Smiling," *Cork Examiner*, Cork, Ireland, May 18, 1983.

Kingston, William J. *The Story of West Carbery.* Waterford, 1985.

Lecky, W.E.H. *A History of Ireland in the Eighteenth Century*, abridged with introduction by L.P. Curtis. Chicago, 1972. See Chapter II, "Religion and Society," pp. 37-114.

Lewis, Samuel. *A Topographical Dictionary of Ireland.* London, 1837.

"Living 100 Years is Attainment of an Oshkosh Woman" About Mary Blake, *Oshkosh Daily Northwestern,* December (day?) 1925 clipping in author's file.

McCourt, Desmond. *The Rundale System in Ireland: A Study of Its Geographical Distribution and Social Relations.* Unpublished doctoral dissertation, Queens University, Belfast, 1950. McCourt's chart showing rundale patterns of land holding in 19th century Ireland can be found on p. 109 of unpublished doctoral dissertation by Patrick Blessing, *West Among Strangers: Irish Migration to California, 1850-1880*, University of California at Los Angeles, 1977.

McDowell, R.B. *Social Life in Ireland 1800-45.* Cork, 1976.

Merriman, Brian. *Cúirt an Mheán-Oíche, The Midnight Court.* Text and translation by Patrick C. Power, Cork, 1977. Quoted passage is from Frank O'Connor's less literal but more spirited translation in *Penguin Book of Irish Verse*, edited with an introduction by Brendan Kennelly. London, 1970, pp. 91-118.

Moore, John. *Diary of John Moore,* edited by Major-General Sir J.F. Maurice. London, 1904.

Moran, Cardinal Patrick. *The Catholics of Ireland Under the Penal Laws in the Eighteenth Century.* London, 1899. Much information on reports from Ireland to Rome and the continent.

Murphy, Father Denis, S.J. *Our Martyrs.* Dublin, 1896.

New Brunswick Census, Northumberland County, North Esk, Nelson, and Derby parishes, years 1851, 1861, 1871, National Archives of Canada, Ottawa, on film. Also, *Return of Assessments,* 1830-34, North Esk Parish. Provincial Archives of New Brunswick, Fredericton, films L95-97.

The O'Mahony Journal, publication of the the O Mahony Records Society, annual, 1971. Cork County Library.

O'Brien, William F., "The Dating of the Mt. Gabriel-type Copper Mines of West Cork," *Journal of the Cork Historical and Archaeological Society,* 1987, pp. 50-70. Latest research.

Ó Cruadhlaoich, Diarmuid. *The Oath of Allegiance.* Dublin & London, 1925, pp. 16-17.

Ó Maidín, Pádraig. "Leamcon Castle and Leamcon House," *Cork Examiner* (undated clipping in author's file), based on the following articles by Arthur E.J. Went: "Sir William Hull's Losses in 1644," *Journal of the Cork Historical and Archaeological Society,* LII (1947), pp. 55-68; "Pilchards in the South of Ireland," *JCHAS,* LI (1946), pp. 137-57; and "Foreign Fishing Fleets Along the Irish Coast," *JCHAS,* LIV (1949), pp. 17-24.

Ó Murchadha, Diarmuid. *Family Names of County Cork.* Dublin, 1985. Information on (O) Mahony families. Also correspondence with author, 1994. See also Holland.

O'Neill, T.P., "Rural Life," in *Social Life in Ireland, 1800-1845* ed. by R.B. McDowell. Cork, 1976.

Ordnance Survey Office, Phoenix Park, Dublin. Maps of West Cork and the parishes of Schull and Kilmoe; West Cork 1/2"=1 mi., sheet 24; West Cork 1"=1 mi., sheets 199, 200, 204, 205 (Schull and parts of Kilmoe parishes); West Schull, 6"=1 mi., sheets 131, 139, 140, 148, 1st ed., c1843.

Parish registers, Goleen and Schull, County Cork, National Library of Ireland, Dublin.

Parish register of St. Patrick's Church, Nelson-Miramichi, New Brunswick.

Parish register of St. Michael's Church, Stillwater, Minnesota.

The Parliamentary Gazetteer of Ireland. Dublin, 1843-46. Information on tithes, the glebe house, and schools in Schull Parish.

Parliamentary Papers. *Report of Commission inquiring into the condition of the poorer classes in Ireland, 1835 and 1836 (Poor Inquiry)*. National Library of Ireland, Dublin.

"Pioneer Logger [Michael Fitzgerald] Celebrates 99th Birthday," *Oshkosh Daily Northwestern*, November 8, 1924, p. 5.

Reilly, A.J. *Father John Murphy: Famine Priest (1796-1883)*. Dublin and London, 1963. Account of Father Murphy's work in Goleen Parish, winning back "soupers" who had been proselytized by W.A. Fisher.

"Report on the State of Popery in Ireland, 1731," in *Archivium Hibernicum*, vol. I (1912), vol. II (1913), vol. III (1914).

Return of the Commissioners appointed to take up the census of Ireland for the year 1841, pp. 171-72 (504), 1843, XXII, No. 1. National Library of Ireland, Dublin.

Return of the Owners of Land....(1876). Information on Richard Edward Hull's landholdings in 1876. Cork County Library.

Roberts, Jack. *Sketches of West Carbery: The Megaliths of West Cork*. Key Books, Skibbereen (undated, c1988).

_____ . *Ancient, Sacred and Historic Sites of West Cork: Map and Guide*. Key Books, Skibbereen (undated, c1988).

Ronan, Myles C. *The Irish Martyrs of the Penal Laws*. London, 1935. Information on 1572-1713 period.

Southern Star, Skibbereen, County Cork, July 3, 1982, account of historic services on the Schull Mass Rock.

Tithe Applotment Books. Schull/Skull and Kilmoe parishes, Barony of West Carbery (West), 1827. National Library of Ireland, Dublin.

Townsend, Rev. Horatio. *A General and Statistical Survey of the County of Cork*, 2nd edition, 2 vols. Cork, 1815, vol. 1, pp. 316-19.

United States Censuses, Winnebago County, Wisconsin, 1860-1880.

Wall, Maureen. *The Penal Laws, 1691-1760*. Dundalk, Ireland, 1967.

Woodham-Smith, Cecil. *The Great Hunger*. London, 1962 and 1970.

Bibliography for Chapter 2: The Exodus to Miramichi, New Brunswick

Adams, William Forbes. *Ireland and Irish Emigration to the New World: from 1815 to the Famine*. New Haven, 1932.

Arbuckle, Doreen M. *The North West Miramichi*. Ottawa, 1978.

Hamilton, W.D. "Early Schools of the Miramichi," *Moncton Times*, Moncton, New Brunswick, December 22, 1977. Also *Old North Esk Revised*, Fredericton, 1988, and *Miramichi Papers*, Fredericton, 1987.

Hoddinott, Rev. D. F. *From Whence We Came*. Newcastle, New

Brunswick, 1978.

Johnston, James. *Notes on North America*, 2 vols. London, 1851.

King, Joseph A. "Bing Crosby's Irish Roots: The Harrigan Family of County Cork, New Brunswick, Minnesota, and Washington," *Irish-American Genealogist*, Augustan Society, Torrance, California, vol. VII, nos. 1-4, issue 29-32, 1983.

_____. *The Irish Lumberman-Farmer*. Lafayette, California, 1982.

_____. "Irish Methodists Sunk Deep Roots Along the Miramichi," "The Miramichi Irish: Returning Timber Ships Supported by Migration," and "Williamstown's First Irish Catholic School Master," a series in *The Times-Transcript*, Moncton, New Brunswick, July 15 and 16, 1986.

Lawrence, Joseph Wilson. *Judges of New Brunswick and Their Times*, edited by D.G. Bell, Fredericton, New Brunswick, 1983.

Mackay, Donald. *Flight from Famine: The Coming of the Irish to Canada*. Toronto and London, 1990. Chapter 9, "Off We Go to the Miramichi" (data on Harrigan and Fitzgerald families taken from King, *The Irish Lumberman-Farmer*).

National Archives of Canada. *New Brunswick Executive Council, Education, Parish, County and Grammar Schools: Correspondence and Petitions, 1819-1856*. File MG 9 A1, vol. 113, pp. 2004-34. Items on Evers Controversy, including North Esk trustees' report of hearings, letter from John Dunnett, Joseph McLean's petitions. Also filed at Provincial Archives of New Brunswick, Fredericton.

New Brunswick Census, Northumberland County, North Esk, Nelson (Northside), Derby, and South Esk parishes, 1851, 1861, 1871, 1881. Nelson (Northside) became Derby Parish, and is so reported on the 1861 census; part of North Esk became South Esk, and is so reported on 1881 census.

Provincial Archives of New Brunswick, Fredericton. *House of Assembly Sessional Records*. Petitions of James Evers and thirteen Williamstown residents, February 4, 1848, RS-24 PE/file 10, 1848; report of school committee, March 15, 1848, FS-24 RE/file 7, 1848; and RS-24/22 files 3 and 5, 1848; Also *Colebrooke Papers*, files RS-345 H8 1848, RS 345-A2 1848, and RS 345-E8 1848; and *Minutes of the Provincial Board of Education*, F-380, May 6, 1848, pp. 5-6 (appointment of three justices of the peace).

Bibliography for Chapter 3: Further West

Curti, Merle. *The Making of an American Community: A Case Study of Democracy in a Frontier County*. Stanford, 1959.

Danky, James P., editor. *Genealogical Research: An Introduction to the Resources of the State Historical Society of Wisconsin*. Madison, 1979.

Notes and Bibliography

Ginke, Hazel. "Fitzgerald Station and Its Neighborhood," c1926. Oshkosh Public Museum manuscript collection.

Holmes, Fred L. *Old World Wisconsin.* Eau Claire, 1944, chapter IX.

Johnston, James. *Notes on North America,* 2 vols. London, 1851.

Keena, Catherine A. "Recollections of Mrs. Mary Blake." Manuscript in Oshkosh (Wisconsin) Public Museum, c1926, 3 pp.

King, Joseph A. *The Irish Lumberman-Farmer.* Lafayette, California, 1982.

McDonald, Grace. *History of the Irish in Wisconsin in the Nineteenth Century.* New York, 1976 (first published 1954).

Nelligan, John. *The Life of a Lumberman.* Madison, 1929.

Riverside Cemetery, Oshkosh. Extensive records by plat on 3x5 cards.

Stephenson, Isaac. *Recollections of a Long Life.* Chicago, 1915, chapter 4.

Sweet, James R. *Genealogy and Local History: An Archival and Bibliographical Guide.* Genealogical Associates, Evanston, Illinois, 1962.

United States Censuses, Wisconsin (state and territory), 1820-1880.

Bibliography for Appendix A: A Genealogical Study: Harrigans and Crosbys

Danaher, Kevin. *Irish Country People.* Cork, 1966.

Griffith's Valuations, Parish of Schull (Skull), Barony of West Carbery (West Division), County Cork, c1848, published 1853.

Hamilton, W. D. *Old North Esk Revised.* Fredericton, New Brunswick, 1988.

King, Joseph A. *The Irish Lumberman-Farmer.* Lafayette, California, 1982. Appendix A, Irish Records. See also for Chapter 1.

_____. "Tracing Bing Crosby's Roots to West Cork," *Southern Star,* Skibbereen, County Cork, June 25, 1983.

_____. "When Irish Eyes Are Smiling," *Cork Examiner,* Cork, Ireland, May 18, 1983.

_____. (with Margaret E. Fitzgerald). *The Uncounted Irish in Canada and the United States.* Toronto, 1990.

New Brunswick Census, Northumberland County, North Esk Parish, 1851, 1861.

Records of the Bing Crosby Historical Society, now at Gonzaga University, Spokane, Washington.

Tithe Applotment Books, Parish of Schull (West Division), County Cork, Ireland, 1827.

Index

Deasy, Fr. John, of Schull, 91
de Beaumont, Gustave, 29
De Danaans, 3
Derby, Ellen, m. Michael
    Fitzgereald, 96
Derby Parish NB, 82
Derryleary townland, 2;
    confiscations, 10; 27, 36,
    85, 105
Devon Commission, 21
Dingle, 37
diocese, definition, 100
Dollard, Bishop William of
    NB, 47, 97
Dominicans, 10, 15
Doneraile, Lord, punishes
    priest, 17
Donovan, 43. *See also*
    O'Donovan.
Donovan, Michael, of Schull,
    85
Doyle, Bishop James of
    Kildare & Leighlin, 30
Drinane townland, 2, 5, 85
    confiscations, 10; 27, 36,
    105
Driscoll, Catherine, 46, 47
Driscoll, Dan, godfather of
    Patrick Harrigan, 93
Driscoll, Michael, godfather
    of John Harrigan, 93
Dunbeacon, 7; rebel raid, 9
Dunboyne Foundation,
    Maynooth, 18
Dunmanus, confiscations, 10
Dunn, Mary, godmother of
    Catherine Harrigan
    Crosby, 95
Dunnett, John, NB school
    trustee, 61, 63-64, 68
Durris, confiscations, 10
Dwellings, appalling
    conditions of, 28-29

Egan, Fr. Michael, of Nelson
    NB, 60
Education, bardic 8; 19, 20,
    31; in NB, 58*ff*
Elizabeth I, Queen, 8
Emmet, Robert, 42
England, 7
English, Fr. Nicholas,
    arrested, 15
Evans, Thomas, of
    Aghadown, tithes
    commissioner, 25
Evanson, Rev. Alleyn, Schull,
    26
Evers, James, NB
    schoolmaster, 50; accused
    of defiling pupils, 59*ff*;
    answers charge, 64-65; 71,
    107

Famine (The Great Famine),
    31*ff*; deaths, Schull and
    Kilmoe, 32*ff*; food amidst
    famine, 36; Soup Kitchen
    Act, 40
Farrell, Joseph, m. Ann
    Fitzgerald, 96
Fayle, Sidney, NB
    schoolmaster, 58
Feeley, James, m. Ellen
    Lucey, 96
Ferguson, William, NB
    schoolmaster, charged with
    indecent behavior, 60
Finin of Rossbrin, 8
Firbolgs, 3
Fisher, Rev. William A.,
    Kilmoe/Goleen, 4, 37*ff*
Fitzgerald, Ann, baptism of,
    47; m. Joseph Farrell, 96
Fitzgerald, Cecil B., mayor of
    Seattle, 74
Fitzgerald, Cornelius, the
    "Cherry King," 74